ISBN 978-1-331-41777-4
PIBN 10187344

This book is a reproduction of an important historical work. Forgotten Books uses
state-of-the-art technology to digitally reconstruct the work, preserving the original format
whilst repairing imperfections present in the aged copy. In rare cases, an imperfection in
the original, such as a blemish or missing page, may be replicated in our edition. We do,
however, repair the vast majority of imperfections successfully; any imperfections that
remain are intentionally left to preserve the state of such historical works.

1 MONTH OF
FREE
READING

at

www.ForgottenBooks.com

By purchasing this book you are eligible for one month membership to ForgottenBooks.com, giving you unlimited access to our entire collection of over 700,000 titles via our web site and mobile apps.

To claim your free month visit: www.forgottenbooks.com/free187344

English
Français
Deutsche
Italiano
Español
Português

www.forgottenbooks.com

Mythology Photography **Fiction**
Fishing Christianity **Art** Cooking
Essays Buddhism Freemasonry
Medicine **Biology** Music **Ancient
Egypt** Evolution Carpentry Physics
Dance Geology **Mathematics** Fitness
Shakespeare **Folklore** Yoga Marketing
Confidence Immortality Biographies
Poetry **Psychology** Witchcraft
Electronics Chemistry History **Law**
Accounting **Philosophy** Anthropology
Alchemy Drama Quantum Mechanics
Atheism Sexual Health **Ancient History**
Entrepreneurship Languages Sport
Paleontology Needlework Islam
Metaphysics Investment Archaeology
Parenting Statistics Criminology
Motivational

S P A R K L E S

OF GLORY.

SPARKLES

OF

GLORY,

OR

Some Beams of the

MORNING STAR.

Wherein are many discoveries
as to *Truth* and *Peace.*

To the establishment and pure enlargement of a Christian in *Spirit*
and *Truth.*

By JOHN SALTMARSH,
Preacher of the *Gospel.*

HOSEA 3.
His coming is prepared as the morning.

LONDON:
Printed in the year 1647.
Reprinted for *William Pickering,*
1847.

THE TABLE.

THE two Creations, or two Natures of Flesh and Spirit   1
The true Church   11
The true Personal Reign of Christ as it is Spiritual   14
Antichrist within us   17
The Doctrine of Baptisms . .   18
The Baptists   18
The Baptism of Sufferings . .   22
The Baptism of Water, or of *John*   23
The Baptism of the Holy Ghost, or Gifts   26
The Baptism of Christ   28
The Divers Ministery, with the Ministery of Christ in his Saints   31
The Passage from lower Ministrations to higher   40
The Spirit and Life of outward Ordinances   55
The Christian under Episcopacy, Prelacy, Presbytery, Baptism, Independency, &c.   61
The Christian in Truth   66
The Witnesses in Sackcloth . .   68
Magistracy a Power ordained of God   88
The discerning of Spirits . . .   91
Principles of War and Peace . .   96

b

The Table.

In order to Peace, and Suffering, and Love:

1. The Will of God . . 99
2. God changing Dispensations 101
3. The Law of Nature and Grace 102
4. The Gospel Method of Victory 103
5. How Resistings in some are of Flesh, and of the Law of Nature in others 104
6. The Advantage Christians have of Bondage . 105
7. Upon what Account the purest and freest outward Liberty is 106
8. A Word concerning Heresy and Schism . . 109
   Heresy 111
   Schism 112
9. Truth 113

The Mystery of true Christian Liberty from God, not from Man, or the Power of Man . 116

A Discovery of the highest Attainment of the Protestants generally in the Mystery of Salvation 118

Of Faith 121

A further Discovery as to Free-Grace 121

A Discovery as to the general Point, or Christ dying for all . 125

The last Discovery, and as some

The Table.

say, the highest and most glorious, concerning the whole Mystery of God to Men, and this Creation 127

An additional concerning Antichrist and the Mystery of Iniquity 133

The several Attainments of the Common Protestant . . . 140

The general Redemptionist . . 140

The Free-Gracian 141

Conclusion 142

A Discovery of Prayer . . . 143

A Discovery of the Law . . . 150

A Discovery of Duties and Works 154

A Discovery of outward Ordinances 156

A Discovery of the Jews, and their Conversion 158

All false Worships and Ways practised in Conscience, or in Liberty, will be destroyed in Christ's Day 160

A Discovery of Christ in us . . 162

The Fiery Trial 163

God in Heaven, or in a Place of Distance, as to our Infirmity . 167

The Spiritual Sabbath 169

The Gospel as in its own Glory, and as in the Scriptures of the Old and New Testament . . 171

Assurance of Salvation . . . 175

The Knowledge of God according to the various Dispensations of Himself 179

The Table.

A further Discovery of the Mystery of Salvation in the Gospel Administration, and its own Glory 182

The Seekers' Attainment, with a Discovery of a more Spiritual Way 185

The Grounds both against Liberty of Conscience, and for it, clearly stated, for all to judge :

Against *Liberty of Conscience*, the strongest Grounds, and all the Grounds generally known 191

The Grounds for *Liberty of Conscience* which are strongest, and are all commonly known 193

A Mystery, or the Christian following the Appearances of God through all created Things . 200

A Postscript to Mr. *Gataker* . 202

A pretended Heresy 206

A short Epistle to Master *Knolls*, the Author of a Book, called The shining of a flaming Fire, &c. written against me, as to the Point of Baptism . . . 208

To the High and Honourable Court of Parliament.

WHAT others have done by the *Law* of your *authority*, *Presented* before ye their *advice* in *matters* of *Religion;* I shall, from the *law* of *love* to your *Just authority*, present ye, not *my advice* (the Lord himself advise and counsel ye) but some *things* which concern the Lord *Jesus Christ*, and the *peace* and *prosperity* of your *Kingdom;* and that I may not be disobedient to the *heavenly vision*, or *light* of God revealed *in me.*

ἐγενόμην ἐκ
ἀπειθής τῇ
ἐρανίῳ ὀπλα-
σίᾳ
Acts 26. 19.

There are two *Principles* in the world which have these sad, and *dark* conclusions *attending* them, the two Principles are these :

1. That such as conform not to the *Doctrine* and *discipline* established; and yet as to the *State* are good *Subjects*, and *peaceably* af-

A

fected, shall be *proceeded* against by *fines, imprisonment, &c.*

2. That such as shall *speak* upon the *Scriptures*, or open them, *Publicly*, or in *Private*, and are not or*dained* by the laying on of the *hands* of that present established *ministery* of a *kingdom*, shall be proceeded against by *fines, imprisonment, &c.*

The *sad* and *dark* conclusions which follow, are these:

1. All the glorious *discoveries* of *God, above,* or *beyond* that *System,* or *form* of *Doctrine, &c.* shall be *judged,* and *sentenced,* as *Heresy* and *Schism;* and so *God* himself shall be *judged* by *man,* which must needs be a *sin,* bringing much *desolation;* unless they that enact such Laws, were that very *infallible Apostleship* for *Interpretation* of all *Scriptures;* as the first *Apostleship* was for *writing* all *Scriptures.* And is *God,*

Rom. 3. 29.
Ιϵδαίων ὁ
ϵϵὸς μόνον;

a *God* of the *Jews* only, is he not a *God* of the *Gentiles* also? that is, is *God* limited to one *sort* of *men?* Thou *thoughtest* (saith God)

Psal. 51.

that *I was altogether,* such *an one* as *thyself;* that is, a *God* merely of one *Image* or *figure*: behold, the *Heaven* of *Heavens* cannot con- Psal. tain him, he dwelleth not in *Temples* made *with hands*, and where is *his habitation*, and who hath *known the place* of his *rest?* That is, what is *man* that he should conceive that *God* is only in a *place*, or *Temple*, or *form* of *Worship*, or *System* of *Doctrine* of his *form* or *making*, since the *time* is come, that we do no longer *worship* in this *Temple*, nor at *Jerusalem*; but John 4. they that *worship*, must *worship* in *spirit* and *truth*; which *truth*, John 14. is he only who is the *truth*.

2. Many thousands of *precious Christians* shall be under *Delinquency*, as to *fines*, *imprisonment*, *&c.* and under the scandal of *Hereties* and *Schismatics*; because not seeing by that *one* light, nor believing in that one *Proportion* of *faith*, nor receiving such *interpretations* and *Consequences* of *Scriptures*, for the very *Scriptures* themselves; and by such *persecution*, the *civil power* which is received from *God*, shall be turned against *God*, or against the more *spiritual administration* of *God;* and so

God's Administrations dashed *one* against *another.*

Acts 9.   *Saul, Saul, why persecutest thou me?* touch not *mine anointed, and*

Psal.   *do my Prophets no harm:* not as *having dominion* over *the heritage,* or *Lordship* over *faith.*

3. That were to set up the *Church Polity* of the *Jews* amongst *Christians;* and not according to *God's divine appointment,* but *man's;* for *God* in that first Polity of the *Jews' Church* under the *Old Testament,* joined to the *Kings* and *Magistracy* then, a *Priesthood* with *Urim* and *Thummim;* and *Prophets anointed* of *God* as a *certain, true, infallible,* directive power for ordering that way of *administration;* but this way of *Christians* now, *without* any such *warrant,* or *appointment* of *God* brings back again the same *Church Polity,* under the *New Testament,* which was typical as to *Christ* the *King* and *Priest,* and *Prophet,* and joins to *Kings* and *Magistracy* now, a *ministery less* of *God,* less certain, less true, not *infallible;* so as all *texts, instances,* and examples brought from the *Old Testament* of the *Kings,*

Princes, and *Magistrates* of *Israel,* *compelling* to the *worship* of *God,* without proving the continuance of the same *Church Polity* under the *New Testament,* and the like *Priesthood,* and *Prophets* accordingly *sent* of *God* to direct them, is all *invalid,* and of no effect as to such *proceedings.*

4. The *infinitely* abounding *spirit* of God, which blows *when* and *where* it *listeth,* and *ministers* in *Christians* according to the *gift,* and *prophesies* according to the *will* of the *Almighty God;* pouring itself out upon all *flesh,* giving out the *word,* and making the *company* great *who publish* it, even this *Almighty,* all *glorious, infinitely abounding, dispensing,* and *revealing* Spirit, is made subject to the *Laws* and *Ordinances* of *men,* to the *pleasures* and *wills,* to the measures and forms of men, to *outward* ceremonies, as Ordination, &c. God must not speak till man give him leave; not teach, nor Preach, but whom man *allows,* and *approves,* and or*dains.*

John 3. 8.
Rom. 12. 6.
Acts 2. 18.
Psal. 68. 11.

Τὸ πνεῦμα ὅπȣ θέλει πνεῖ ἔτι δȣλȣς μȣ, ἐπὶ δȣλας μȣ ἐκχέω ἀπὸ τȣ πνεύματος μȣ.

5. This making *laws* for punishing all that con*form* not to the

doctrine and *discipline* established, destroys the true interests of all *states* and *kingdoms*, excluding all *societies* of men, but of one *sort* and *form*, though never so peaceably *affected*, or obedient *as men* and *Subjects*, respectively to the *State*, and civil *government* thereof, and was never found in any *State*, or *Church Polity* by *divine* appointment, but in that one *nation* of the *Jews*, whose *Polity*, as to such a form, God himself peculiarly made, owned and preserved, and the *Lord Jesus* himself *fulfilled* and dissolved.

For *Heresy* and *Schism*, I know ye ought not to tolerate any, but to let them bear their *own judgment*, which is spiritual *admonition*, *Church-censure*, *rejection*, *excommunication*; which if *effectual*, as all *true*, *right*, *spiritual* censures have been and are, is that *just proportionable judgment* for such Gospel-sins; if not *effectual*, then the *insufficiency*, *weakness*, *unprofitableness* of *such* as assume such *Church-power*, and *censures*, will appear before ye.

And as to that *point* of the pre-

Tit. 3. 10.
1 Cor. 5. 5.
2 Thes. 3.
15.
παραδῦναι τὸν τοιῦτον πῶ σατανᾶ. ἁιρετικον ἄν 3ρωπον παραιτῶ νυθετέιτε.

sent *Ordination*, which some have *so pressed* upon ye, distinguishing to ye, that their *Ordination* was from the *Bishops*, as *Ministers*, not as *Bishops*. *Right Honourable*, consider, that distinction cannot be, for there was no such thing as *Ministers* in the *Church* of *Rome*, or of *England* as to this successively pretended *Ordination;* but *Priests*, and *Bishops*, or *Episcopacy*, and *Priesthood:* and surely if *Episcopacy* doth not, yet *Priesthood* doth altogether *evacuate* the essence of *Ministery* now under the *New Testament* as by such *Ordination:* and how much more *rational* are their Arguments, who hold their *Ministery lawful*, from the *lawfulness* of *Episcopacy;* than those, who deny *Episcopacy*, *&c.* and yet have no *Ordination* but from them.

See *Mason.* *Fox*'s Book of Martyis. *Beda.*

For this *Christian-liberty*, it is such as preserves not only the outward *peace* of *Christians* who enjoy it, but the *peace* and *prosperity* of *Kingdoms*, and *Magistrates*, who *establish* it; and the *life*, *glory*, and *happiness*, *destruction*, and *death* of *Kingdoms* is wrapped in

Eph. 5. 30.
Acts 9. 4.
Mal. 3.
Psal. 105.
15. the *Christian's life* or *death :* they are the *parts* and *Members* of Christ, the *apple* of *his eye*, his *Jewels*, his *anointed*, his *Prophets*, his *Children.*

As therefore ye look to be prospered by this *Spirit of God ;* as ye look for *wisdom* from this *Spirit* of *God* to govern this State ; as ye look for comfort from this *Spirit* of *God* in all your *distresses ;* as ye look for *gifts* from this *Spirit* of *God* in all the *administrations :* as ye look for the sweet *spiritual breathings* and *refreshments* from this *Spirit* of *God* in all the several *changes* of this *creation : love, preserve, Indulge* this *Spirit ; quench* not, *oppose* not, *oppress* not this Spirit : confine it not to one outward form or fellowship of men,

1 Thes. 1.
5. 19.
Acts 7. 51.
Eph. 4. 10. which are not that Catholic Church, that *Apostleship* of *infallibility ;* and they that are *spiritual*, live in that *spirit* and *truth*, which

John 8. 32,
36.
ἡ ἀλήθεια
ἐλευθερώσει
ὑμᾶς. makes them *free indeed*, and it is below that *Spirit of God*, to *Petition liberty* of conscience in *spirituals*, from any *men* or *Magistrates* in the World ; because God *will make Jerusalem a cup of trem-*

bling to all *Nations,* and a *stone* of *astonishment ;* and the spiritual *Christians* will rather hold forth such things, to bear witness to the *truth,* and to desire all to forbear *persecution,* as much for *their own* sakes who *persecute,* as for *theirs* who are *persecuted.*

And for that just *power* of *Magistracy,* I acknowledge it a *Power* Ordained of *God,* for *administration* of *Justice* and *righteousness* in the *societies* of men, and *nations ;* a *Minister* of *God* for *good,* a *terror* to evil *works ;* and that we are to be *subject to every Ordinance of man,* for the *Lord's sake ;* and for this cause we *pay tribute to whom tribute ; honour to whom honour :* and all *societies* of *Christians* by no *pretence* of *religion,* or liberty for the worship of God, are to *resist* or *disturb* the civil *administration* of this *power :* but as to that consideration ; all *Christians* are to *suffer* according to the *will* of *God,* (all lawful ways for *preservation* of *States* and *Kingdoms* still excepted) and all such *Magistracy* are to preserve their respective *States,* by all *wholesome, lawful,* cautionary

ἀπὸ τῦ Θεῦ τεταγμήναι εἰσιν. Rom. 13. 1, 2, 3.

Rom. 13. 4, 5. τῷ τὸ τέλος τὸ τέλος, τῷ φόρον τῷ φόρον.

A 2

Laws and *Ordinances*, in *Peace;* so as while *liberty* or *indulgency*, as to the *tender consciences* in Religion is spoken on, yet no less *security* of the *State*, no *diminution* to the just power of *Magistracy ;* no less *preservation* of the *Peace* of the *Kingdom* is desired by those that are truly *spiritual.* And though many suffer under the *name* of *Heretics* and *Schismatics* before ye, for not conforming to the present *doctrine* and *discipline established ; Right Honourable*, consider, whether this doth not call in question all the very present *doctrine* and *discipline* so established; for by this very thing of judging all *Inconformity* to the present *worship* and *form* of *things* to be *Heresy ;* by the same, all this present *form* of *worship* and *confession of faith* is judged *Heresy* and *Schism*, to the late *former* government, and *doctrine* established in the Church of England: this present *Synod of men* being no more that visible *Catholic Church*, and *infallible Apostleship*, than the former were, so as the changing the former *Articles* of the *Church* of *England* into a new *confession* of *faith*, the *Episcopacy* into *Presbytery* ; and so altering both the *fundamentals* in re*ligion* and the *discipline*, is equally *new light* and *Heresy*, as to the former *doctrine* and *discipline* : (and if it be objected) but this present *Synod*, are men of more *light* and *Piety* than the *former*, and so they establish more *truth*, and bring in more *Reformation* ; if so, why is there not more *love*, more *peaceableness*, more *self-denial*, more *power* of *godliness*, than there was in the suffering *Bishops*, and the Preaching *Lay-Martyrs* then ; who loved *Christ* in *himself*, and in one another.

And now (*Noble Senators*) since *very worthy things have been formerly done by ye* unto this *Nation ;* let not your *Sun* set in a *cloud*, nor your *light* shine upon those that have *loved* you, as the *Moon* once upon the *Water*, making it of the co*lour of Blood ;* are *ye not* come to the *Kingdom* in *Peace?* Are not the *gleanings* of *Ephraim* in the *Vintage?* Did not *David* say, *shall* any *man be put to death this day in Israel?* 2 Sam. 19. 22.

The Lord enlighten ye (if it be
his will) more and more, in the
knowledge of *Jesus Christ*, and of
the *love* of *God*, and of *all* who
have any *thing* of *God* in *them*, and
let you see those things *which concern your peace in* this your day.

Your Honours' humble

Servant,

JOHN SALTMARSH.

To all true Christians.

FRIENDS,

THE only *scope* of *this Book*, is to mind ye of an higher *excellency*, than mere *created things* can afford *ye*, of the *truth* as it is in *Jesus*, or in *Spirit*.

And of that *unity* of *Spirit* which *Christians* should live in, under their several *forms* and *attainments*, and I have not held forth any *discovery* of *truth*, or of any higher dispensation, so as to *darken* too much other *dispensations* in which *Christians* live, or to lessen and undervalue their *attainments*, but only to be *faithful* in the *power* of *God* to his *discoveries* in my own spirit.

I desire we may all *bear* one another's *burdens*, and consider, that God is in all his several *Dispensations*, and *measures*, and *Christians* are not to hasten out of any till the

Lord himself say, *C*ome up hither; and the *stronger* are to bear the *infirmities* of the *weak*.

I am not against the *Law*, nor repentance, nor *duties*, nor ordinances, as some would say: So as all these flow from their right *principle*, to their right *end*.

I am not against the settling of *Church-Government Prudentially*, as now, so as all of another *way* be not persecuted. Because I know *God* hath his *people* under several *attainments* and *measures*, and is to his *people* in all *these*, in his mere *grace* and *love*, as formerly to the *Bishops* and *thousands* of weak *C*hristians in Queen *Elizabeth*'s, and Queen *Mary*'s days of *Martyrdom*, in their forms.

I am only against any form, as it becomes an engine of *persecution* to all *Christians* differing from it.

I am not against the *sitting* of an *Assembly* or *Synod* at *Westminster*, that are so persuaded, because, that is but to allow such liberty to others' *consciences*, as we desire ourselves; and surely if they would propound such things only as they have re*ceived*, or they are in *co*ns*cie*nce persuaded of to all the *Kingdom;* and so leave it to the *Spirit of God* and their *mi-nistery* to *persuade* and co*nvince* all others, and not desire power from others to co*mpel;* this were but to *minis*te*r* as they had received.

I have stated some *things*, and *truths*, as they are held in those very grounds ; the Spirit of *God* in the Reader may judge *truth* without any determination of man.

I have spoken concerning the *li-berty* of some that are *spiritual* in outward things of *worship* and *dis-cipline* without *sin*, yet of no other, but as the *wisdom* of *God* shall di-rect to *edification*, and with care of *offence*, and *Scriptures* allow : *To the weak I became as weak; to them that were under the Law, as under the Law; to them that were without Law, as without Law, though not without Law to God.* 1 Cor. 9. 22. Now in this *Scripture*, liberty to things of former *institution* by God, and of no such *institution*, is discovered ; those words, *under the Law*, contain *liberty* to things o*n*ce *instituted,* and those .words, *with-out Law,* to things not *instituted,*

1 Cor. 8. 4, 7.

and therefore the *Apostle* saith, *We know, an Idol is nothing, Howbeit, there is not in every man that know-ledge;* and again,

Mat.

To the pure all things are pure, and that *that goes into the man, defiles not the man.*

And yet I know this very truth, as well as that of the *grace of God,* and all other *truths* may be turned into *wantonness,* and *licentiousness,* and not pure *Christian liberty.*

I am for the *knowledge* of *God* in the Father, Son, and Spirit, and for true *C*hristianity, as it is in *life,* and *Spirit,* and *power* of *god-liness,* and for *love* to all; but to

Phil. 3. 3.

the *sins* of *all, We are circumci-sion, which worship God in the* Spirit, *and* rejoice *in Christ Jesus, and have no confidence in the Flesh.*

I have spoken of the *true Chris-tian* under that more gross *form* of *Episcopacy,* not approving that *form,* but in order to *higher* and more *spiritual discoveries;* and this I do, because I find *God* in *lower* as well as *higher,* in *purer*

as well as more corr*upt adminis-*
trations; and in *tenderness* and re-
spect to many thousands in this
Kingdom, and many *other King-*
doms, who are not yet out of this
form, and yet *God* may be in them,
as in *Germany, Sweeden, Den-*
mark, in *England* formerly and of
late, God having his more spiritual
times for *them,* as well as o*thers.*

I have spoken of *things* here
sometimes very *briefly,* because I
find less of *man* in writing the *sub-*
*stan*ce and *truth* of things, so far
as revealed in us, than in tedious
discourses and *Paraphrases,* which
are many times rather the works of
reason, and *wit,* and *art,* than of
the *Spirit* of *God;* and I have writ
not in that *common method* of men,
because I received it not accordingly.

I find *two* things which make
some o*utward Ordinances* so exceedingly, and in *divine right* stood
for: the one is, an *opinion,* that
there is a *very model* in the *Letter*
of Scriptures to be discovered;
which is to reduce *Christians* to
bondage again, and to a *form* with-

out those very *gifts*, which is not to be found in the *word*.

The other *opinion* is, that the setting up such a *form*, is an immediate way of *fixing God*, and his *Spirit* upon it, which indeed is a finer kind of *Idolatry*, to conceive that God enters into *outward things*, and conveys his all *glorious*, and *Almighty Spirit* by them, whenas they are only *signs, figures*, and *Images* of more *spiritual* things enjoyed, or to be enjoyed; and that of God's *appearance* and *conveyance* of himself in *outward things*, according to this opinion, is such as the *Papists* hold, as to *Images*, and to things conferring *grace Ex* opere *operato*, and all *Idolaters* accordingly, conceiving that God immediately *informs*, and *glorifies*, and *spiritualizes* those *forms*, and *figures* to the *beholders;* as the *Israelites* when the *Calf* was made, cried, these are thy *Gods O Israel.*

I know *Ordinances* used in their true *nature*, and as things that are the *Parables, figures*, and *types* of *spiritual* things, are not to be rejected, but many *Christians* do sweetly partake of them in this their state of *weakness* and *bondage,* wherein *God* makes *heavenly* things appear by *earthly,* that men, as *Thomas,* may *see* and *believe, though blessed are they that have not seen, and yet do believe.*

All I have now to say to ye is this :

Something of a mystery of *God,* and something of a mystery of *Satan.*

That of *God* is this, that the *Lord* doth in much wisdom suffer the weakness of some *spiritual* men to come forth : and by this, he carries *spiritual* things in more *mystery,* and manages the glory of his *spirit* through *ways* and *things* which are an *offence,* and scandal before the World ; by which some *stumble* and *fall,* and are *broken, Christ* was *set up for the falling as well as rising of many in Israel.*

That of Satan is this, to observe how he fortifies corrupt nature against the *spirit* of *God ;* which *spirit* he knows can only *destroy* his *Kingdom,* and *reveal* the *Kingdom* of *God ;* and therefore counterfeits the *spirit* by false *Revela-tions* and *appearances; transform-ing* himself into an *Angel* of *light*, and then casting all this as a *scan-dal*, upon the pure *Spirit* of *God* by reproaches, *viz.* of *praying* by the *spirit*, and *preaching* by the *spirit*, and new *Revelations*, and new *Light*, thus making the *world blaspheme*, and the *weaker Saints* afraid of the *glory* of the *spirit*, lest it prove a *delusion*.

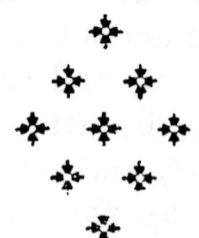

SPARKLES OF GLORY.

The Two Creations or Two Natures of Flesh and Spirit.

THESE two *Creations* are two distinct *Natures*, from whence all things of *Flesh* and *Spirit* come forth ; the two *Adams* are the two seeds, roots, or *principles* of these two *Natures* or *Creations*, the *Old* and *New;* so as in the knowledge of these two there opens a Prospect both of heaven and earth, of the first *man* and the *second,* who are the *sean* or *womb* of all things *carnal* and *spiritual,* and into whom are gathered up all the *Mystery* of *Christ* and *Antichrist,* and from whence the *Mystery* of

πρῶτος ἄνθρω-
πος.

δεύτερος ἄν-
θρωπος.
Eph. 4. 22,
23.

1 Cor. 15.
22.
παλαιὸν ἄν-
θρωπον
καινὸν ἄνθρω-
πον.

B

πνευματικὸς ἀνακρίνει πάντα. both are brought forth before those that are *spiritual;* the *spiritual man judgeth all things.*

The first *Adam* is the root of all fleshly *Creation* and *Excellency;* the *glory* of the first *Creation* is gathered up into him, as the *light* into the *body* of the Sun; the life of *Angels* or *Spirits,* of *sense* or *beasts,* of *nature* or *vegetation,* is all in him : So as *man* is all created excellency in the *map* or *abridg-*

Rev. 21. 3. *ment;* and *God,* making his *Ta-bernacle* with man, dwells at the

ἡ σκηνή τῦ θεῖ μεῖὰ τῶν ἀνθρώπων. same time with all his *Creation; Man,* being the glorious and bright *sum* or *whole* of the *Creation,* was

Rom. 5. 14. *ἐςὶ τύπος.* a *figure* and *type* of the *Son of God,* Jesus *Christ*: And therefore he was said to be made after his

Gen. 1. 26. *ἀπαύγασμα τῆς δόξης.* own *Image,* which Image was *Jesus Christ,* called by the Apostle the *Image of the invisible God,*

Heb. 1. 3. the *brightness of his glory,* and *express Image of his Person.*

And while man was thus in the *Image of God,* and stood and lived in *Communion* with God, walking in that *Paradise,* or that *Glory* of his first *Creation,* in obedience to God, and *participation* of God, he was the *Image* of all or any *created excellency*, as it was, or is, or shall be in order to a more *excellent life*, to a *life* out of itself, in *him* who is the *fountain of life.*   Psal. 36. 9.

And while *man* was in this *communion* and dependency to *God*, as he was made in his *Image*, or as he was the *likeness* and *similitude* of *God*, he was the *figure* and *image* of *Jesus Christ* in his *New Creation*, or *whole body*, or *Saints*, who know no other *life* than in *God, whose springs are all in* him; the *Lord God* being their *everlasting light*, and their *God* their *glory.*   Gen. 1. 26.

Eph. 4. 23. κατὰ θεὸν κτισθέντα.

While they, like the *golden Candlestick* in *Zechariah*, are fed with the *golden oil* that is continually *flowing* and issuing through the *golden pipes.*   Zec. 4. 12.

The excellency of this first *Creation* is but *earthly* or *fleshly* in the *Spirit's* account, and as it stands in distinction to the second *Creation*, or new man, or *Lord* from heaven; so as the circuit or furthest attainment of man in this *Creation* is but to things of this *Creation;* from things of *rational*   1 Cor. 15. 47. πρῶτος ἄνθρωπος ἐκ γῆς, ὁ κύριος ἐξ ὀρανῶ.

and *Angelical* glory to things of *lowest* and most *earthly* life or excellency, of which *Solomon* was an Image: as his heart was *large like the sand on the sea shore*, and as he was *wise* from the *Cedar in Lebanon* to the *wormwood in the wall;* from the highest to the *lowest part* of this Creation, comprehending all from the *top* of this Creation to the *bottom;* and seeing the *face* of *God* in this more darkly, as in a glass, the *invisible things* of him *being clearly seen and understood by the things that are made, even his eternal power and Godhead.*

τὰ ἀόρατα.
Rom. 1. 20.
αἴδιος αὐτᾶ
δύναμις καὶ
θειότης.

Now all this *excellency* and *glory* of the *first man* did leave *God*, being tempted of the *woman* and the *serpent*, which were a figure of *fleshly wisdom* without *God*, and of the *weakness* of this Creation in its own *nature*, as it was drawn away and enticed from its *life* in *God* and *communion* with *God*, to live in *itself*, or own *life*, and to be to *itself* what *God* should have been, *wisdom*, and life, and *righteousness, power*, and *strength*, and preservation, and all things.

Gen. 3.

And as it left *God*, *life*, and *communion* in him, was a *figure* or *image* of this *Creation* departing from *God*, and living out of *God;* and now, according to this *Independent* subsistence or *life* from *God*, it *apostates* and *degenerates* into that *nature* which is called the *seed* of the *serpent*, the *old man*, the *mystery* of *iniquity*, which appeared all along in the cursed *figures* or *types* of *Cain*, of *Esau*, of *Ishmael*, of the children of the *bondwoman*, of *Judas*, of *Antichrist*, of the *whore of Babylon;* so as all the *knowledge* of *sin*, of all *fleshly abominations*, whether more *spiritual* or *carnal*, are discovered in the knowledge of this *first man*, thus discovered as he lives not in *God*, nor in *communion* with *God*, and lives a *life* distinct from the *life* in *God*, and all his *actings* and *workings* are from his own *life*, his *life* of this *Creation*, and to *himself*, not from *God*, nor to *God*.

The second *Adam*, or Jesus Christ, is that *quickening Spirit*, or *Lord from heaven*, and is the root of all the second or new *Creation*, which is *created according to*

2 Thes. 7.
τὸ μυστήριον τῆς ἀνομίας
a ο]lιjo Is.
Gen. 4. u.
παιδίσκης τέκνα.
Gal. 4. 23.
τὴν πόρνην μεγάλην ἔφθειρε.
Rev. 19.

God, *in righteousness and true*
holiness, which *righteousness* is
called the *righteousness of God*
and true holiness, which is an *ho-*
liness more glorious than the *holi-*
ness of the first *Creation,* an *holi-*
ness which is of God, not of man,
and therefore *true holiness,* or *ho-*
liness in truth.

This Jesus, or *second Adam,* as
he is *Spirit,* is called the *Image* of
the *invisible* God, the *brightness*
of his glory, and *express Image of*
his Person; is the *life* manifested,
the *Word of God,* he *that is alive*
for evermore, the *Alpha and Ome-*
ga, the *beginning* and the *ending;*
this is he who is the *wisdom, mind,*
or *understanding* of God, and was
in God, and is the *Immanuel,* or
God with us, or *God* making his
Tabernacle with *men.*

This Jesus Christ is that *glory*
of God in which the *Father* is revealed, and so none knows the
Father but *the Son, and he to*
whom the Son will reveal him.

This is he who, being in the
bosom of God, declares him to the
sons of men, and so *rejoices in the*
habitable parts of the earth.

Eph. 4. 24.
ἐν δικαιοσύνῃ
κὶ ἁγιότητι
ἀληθείας.

εἰκὼν τᾶ θεῦ.
Col. 1. 15.

1 John 1. 2.
ζωὴ ἐφατε-
ρώθη.
John 1. 1.
Rev. 1. 8.

Prov. 8.

Mat. 1. 23.

Rev. 21. 3.

Luke 10.
22.

John 1. 18.

Prov. 8. 31.

This Jesus Christ is the *revelation* of *God*, even the *Father;* this is the *glass* or *crystal* of *God*, in whom *we with open face behold,* as *in a glass, the glory of the Lord*, and are changed from *glory* to *glory.*
2 Cor. 3. 18. *κατοπ]ειζόμε·νοι.*

The *Sons of men* taken into this *glory* of the *Son of God*, are that new or second Creation, that *new Jerusalem*, which came down from God, the ci*ty of the living God,* the *Spirits of just men* made *perfect,* the *new* crea*ture,* the *heavenly men;* as is the *Lord from heaven*, so are they that are *heavenly ;* the *spiritual* men of him who is the *quickening Spirit ;* so as Jesus Christ is made unto us the wisdom, power, righteousness, sanctification, and redemption of God.
Rev. 21. 2. *πόλις θεᾶ ζῶν-7ος.* Heb. 12. 23.
1 Cor. 15. 47, 48.
1 Cor. 15. 45.
1 Cor. 1. 30.

This *Jesus Christ* is the *root, seed, principle,* or ori*ginal* of all this *new* and *heavenly life, glory,* and *spirit* to the *Sons of men,* wherein they enter within the *veil* or *flesh,* which is the first *Creation,* beyond which is this *glory* and *light ;* the veil of this first *Temple* or *Creation* being rent by

him who crucified all *flesh* through
the *eternal Spirit,* and entered
into *his glory,* and is now passed
into the *holiest,* through whom we
have access to God even the *Father,* through the *blood* of the
everlasting Covenant; which *blood*
was the first *Creation* and *Excelleney* crucified to the very *life* and
blood of it; this was the *seal* or
mark of the *New Testament* in
his *blood.*

This *Son* of *God* is he who came
to restore the first *Creation* from
its enmity to God, and so in that
Ministery of his *flesh* became the
word of reconciliation, by which
the *world was* reconciled *unto*
him; and in this *Creation* wherein
man had sinned and departed from
God, living in his own *life,* the
Son of God was manifested in this
Creation to condemn *sin* in the
flesh, and to take away sin, and to
fulfil the *righteousness of the Law*
in the flesh of this first Creation,
the law being weak through the
flesh; and thus he was made *sin*
for us, who knew no sin, that we
might be made the righteousness
of God in him; not only *righte-*

Heb. 9. 14.
Luke 24. 26.
ἐισέλθειν ἐις τὴν δόξαν ἀυῖϛ.

ἐν ἅιματι διαθήκης ἀιωνίϛ.

Cor. 5. 18.
τὴν διακονίαν τῆς καταλλαγῆς.

Rom. 8. 3.

Rom. 8. 3.

ousness according to the *law, Christ being the end of the law (for righteousness) to every one that believeth;* but *the righteous-ness of God,* a righteousness of more *glory* and *excellency.*

Rom. 3. 21, 22. δικαιοσύνη τᾶ θεᾶ.

The *Son of God* did not only fulfil this, bringing home this first *Creation* or *man* to God, accord-ing to his first *excellency* and com-munion with *God;* but in this ap-pearance in the *flesh* he was a *figure* of *God,* whose design is to make his *Saints* his *Temple,* his *Tabernacle,* his *Body,* his *new Creation,* his *new creatures,* his *habitation* or *house.* And God thus *manifested in flesh* was a *figure* of that mystery of *godliness* in us, or God becoming an *Im-manuel; or God with us.*

1 Cor. 6. 19. Rev. 21. 3. 1 Cor. 12. 12. Eph. 4. 24. Eph. 2. 22. θεὸς ἐφανερώθη ἐν σαρκὶ. 1 Tim. 3. 16. Mat. 1. 23.

And in his *crucifying* all this *first glory* in which he appeared, revealed that old design of God, that *mystery hid from ages,* and now made *manifest* to the *Saints;* nailing all the flesh of his *Saints* to the same *Cross,* and *being lifted up* draws *all men unto him,* which is the Mystery of the *Gospel,* or *Christ crucified;* all the *life* or

Col. 1. 26. τὸ μυστήριον τὸ ἀποκεκρυμμέ-νον ἀπὸ τῶν αἰώνων.

excellency of this first *Creation*
being crucified in the *Saints* as in
Christ, whereby they *enter into
their glory* as he did into *his,* and
are in the same *glory* of God made
one, as he and the *Father are
one.*

John 17.
21.

This is that *fellowship of Christ's
death, sufferings* and *resurrection,*
spoken of by *Paul,* into which the
Christian is received.

Phil. 3. 10.
τὴν κοινωνίαν
τῶν παθημά-
των.

And now all things of this *new*
or *second Creation,* as they are
spiritual and *heavenly,* are only
in and through the *same Spirit,* and
discerned in the *same Spirit.*

And the whole *Christ,* or *Son*
of *God,* is *head* and *body, he* and
his, who shall enjoy and live with
God in one *Spirit,* when *God shall
be all in all,* and the *fulness* of
the *stature of Christ* grown up to
be the body of *him who filleth all
in all.*

1 Cor. 12.
12.

ἐν ἐςι σῶμα
ὅτως ὁ Χριςὸς.

Eph. 1. 23.

And Jesus Christ in this consideration of the *whole man,* nature,
or body in which God is revealed,
*is the beginning of the Creation
of God,* the *first-born of every*
creature, in whom *all things sub-
sist.*

τὸ πλήρωμα
παντα ἐν
πᾶσι πληρω-
μένε.

Rev. 3. 14.
Col. 1. 15.
Col. 1. 17.

The true Church.

THAT is the Church or *body* of *Christ* which is *baptized* by one *Spirit* into *oneness* and *unity* of Spirit, a *unity* or incorporation with *Christ*, being *made perfect in one ;* even one, as *thou, Father, art in me, and I in thee.* εἰς ἕνσῶμα ἐβαπτίσθημεν.

John 17. 23.

This *body* is that wherein all the *members live,* and are *quickened* in *one* and the same *Spirit* with Christ, and *in this unity if* one member *suff*er, *all the members suffer with it.*

1 Cor. 12. 13.

1 Cor. 12. 26.

All the members of this body *have the same care one of another.* This body is *spiritual,* and all the members of it *spiritual ;* because Christ is the head of it, and he is a *quickening* Spirit, and the *Lord that Spirit.*

1 Cor. 12. 25.

1 Cor. 11. 3.

2 Cor. 3. 17.

ὁ κύριος. τὸ πνεῦμα.

That is the true Church which is the *Temple* of *God,* where *God* dwells : ye are the *Temples of the Holy Ghost,* Jesus Christ is the *chief* corner *stone* of this Temple, *elect* and *precious ;* this is the *Temple* which the *Angel* measures with a golden reed, and the *Altar*

Eph. 2. 20.
1 Pet. 2. 6.
Rev. 11. 1, 2.

thereof, or the *eternal Spirit*, upon
which all the first *Creation* is offered in the Saints as it was offered in *Christ*, who through the
Heb. 9. 14. *eternal Spirit offered himself,*
leaving out the *outward court*, or
the *flesh* and *first Creation*, and
all outward *administrations*, which
are given to the *Gentiles* to tread
down.

The *Tabernacle* and *Temple*
were *figures* of this wherein *God*
and the *glory* of *God* appeared;
and all *gatherings*, *Communions*,
or *Fellowships* called *Churches* in
the Gospel, were clearer *types* of
this.

ϛύλος. ἑδραί-   This is the *Church* which is the
υμα.   ι
1 Tim. 3. *pillar and ground of truth*, the
15. *general Assembly and Church of*
Heb. 12. *the first born*, which are *written*
23. *in heaven.*

This is the *Church* to which
Jesus Christ is all, and *in all*,
Eph. 4. 11. *filling all*, the *Apostle* to this
Church, the *Prophet*, *Pastor*, and
Teacher, *preaching* to it, *prophe-
sying* in it, *feeding* it, and *watching*
over it, and *teaching* it, so as all
are *taught* of *God*.

This is the *Church* against which

the gates of hell cannot prevail, having Jesus Christ *its rock and foundation.*

Mat. 16. 18. ἔπι ταύτῃ τῇ πέτρᾳ οἰκοδομήσω μῶ τήν ἐκλησίαν.

This is the *Church* to which all the promises of *Spirit, life,* and *glory* are made to the *believers* and *members* that are in this Fellowship and of this Church.

And into this Church all are admitted through the *Spirit* of Christ, and all are discerned *members* in the *same Spirit,* and tried by the *Spirit.*

1 Cor. 12. 10. 1 John 4. 1. δοκιμάζετε τὶ πνεύματα.

And this Church of Christ being thus *baptized by Spirit* into one *body,* is not to be divided by any outward things which are of this *Creation,* which are *visible, outward,* and *perishing;* or by any *fellowship* and *ordinances* below the *glory* of the *Spirit,* which are part of the first *Tabernacle;* nor are the members of this *spiritual Church* to be divided by any *schism* or *division,* procured or effected by any *principle* less, or less excellent than the *Spirit* of *God.*

Col. 2. 20, 21.

And therefore whatsoever *fellowship* in pretence of *Church-notion,* or *Baptism-notion,* or *Presbyterial-notion,* shall cast itself into any *model* of the *letter*, which allows not *communion* with other believers in *Spirit*, in whom the power of the *Spirit*, and of *Christ* cannot be denied, but to be visible and apparent, though not in the practice of some particular ordinance, such *fellowship* will in the *day* of the *Lord Jesus*, or clearer *revelation* of *Christ*, see how they have offended many *little ones*, whom in these outward things they ought to have *pleased to edifica-*

Rom. 13. 10.   *tion*, the *law* of love, and *spirit* or
Rom. 8. 2.   *life* being more royal and excellent,
Col. 2. 20.   than any worldly rudiment whatsoever.

The true Personal Reign of Christ as it is Spiritual.

THE Lord Jesus is entered *into his glory*, having crucified flesh, and
Luke 24.   sits at the *right hand of God*, or in the *choicest glory* of the *Father*,
2 Cor. 3. 17.   where he is the *Lord that Spirit*, and the *Lord of glory*.
1 Cor. 5. 25.   The *Lord Jesus* must reign till he hath put *all his enemies under his feet*: he fills all administrations of *Dominion*, *Judgment*, *Power*, and *Magistracy*, in the world, which

is part of his Kingdom here, all *judgment and power in heaven and earth being committed unto him;* yet this is not his *spiritual reign,* though administered by him who is in *Spirit.*

John 5. 22, 27.
Mat. 28. 18.

The Lord Jesus hath a *kingdom inward* and *spiritual,* the *kingdom of God is within you,* the *kingdom of God is righteousness, peace, and joy,* the *kingdom of God is in power.*

Luke 17. 21.

1 Cor. 4. 20.

The Lord Jesus denied his *kingdom* to *be of this world,* or to come with *observation, as lo here,* or *lo there,* as the *glory* of the *world,* and the *kingdoms* of the *world* is in its appearance.

Luke 17. 21.
Mat. 24.

The Lord Jesus his coming is as *lightning* from *East to West,* filling heaven; lightning is a *glory* without figure, so shall Christ's coming and *revelation* in *Spirit* be; for as the *lightning lighteth from one end of heaven to the other,* so shall the coming of the *Son of man* be.

Mat. 24 27.

The Lord Jesus *his coming* is *in Spirit* and *glory,* in *revelation* in his *Saints;* he shall come *to be glorified in his Saints, and admired in all them that believe.*

2 Thes. 1. 10.

The Lord Jesus reigns already,

all things are *put in subjection under him,* death, and hell, *and sin, and Antichrist, and the* Heb 2. 8. *wicked; only we see not all yet put under him.* Jesus Christ reigns in *Spirit,* only his reign appears not yet; now *are we the* 1 John 3. 1. *Sons of God, but it doth not appear what we shall be ; but when he shall appear, we shall be like him.*

All the *prophecies,* and *promises* of glory, and a *kingdom* of Antichrist to be destroyed, of the *great Battles,* of the *Thrones,* of the *new Jerusalem,* of him on the *white horse,* the *Lord* of *Lords,* and *King* of *Kings* are most glorious in Spirit, and most suitable to *Christ* in the *glory* of his *Father,* and for any other figure of *Christ's* reign or *kingdom,* in any *fleshly* glory, *political* or *monarchical* kingdom, according to any *pattern* upon *earth;* these conceptions or notions are occasioned by the *Allegories,* and *Allusions,* and *Parables* the *Spirit* speaks ; which they that are weak and carnal, as some *Disciples* and *Pharisees* were, take more in the *Letter* than in the *Spirit.*

Antichrist within us.

THAT *Antichristian mystery* which seems to be working in so many *figures* and *shapes* without in the *world*, and makes up the truth of those Scriptures of the *beast*, and the *whore*, and the *false prophet*, &c. flows only from the *Antichrist* within us, or the *mystery of iniquity* which lies in the *flesh*, or *old man*, or *man of sin*, 2 Thes. 2 3. the *Son of perdition*, as in the root, *seed*, or *principle;* and in us you may find all the *delusions* and *deceivableness* of *unrighteousness*, with all the several figures it appears in, in the *Revelation*, and Epistle to the *Thessalonians*, and the Spirit of that *N*atural man in 2 Thes. 2. us acts all that wickedness in us, which in the World comes forth only in *Images* more *Visible*, and *fleshly :* and to the destruction of this Antichrist we should look, and lay the Axe to the root of the tree, carnal wisdom, self-righteousness, high imaginations, fleshly apprehensions of God and Christ, changing the truth of God into a lie, with

all the false testimonies of our own
spirits for the Spirit of God, the
counterfeit *sealings* and *assurances*
of our carnal hearts, the deceivableness of carnal reason, with all other
actings of the flesh.

The Doctrine of Baptisms.

Βαπλίσμων
διδαχὴ.

THE *Doctrine* of *Baptisms* is
such a doctrine as clearly and
spiritually understood, and opened,
will establish the Spirits of many
Christians, who are much in the
dark in these, not distinguishing
Eph. 4. 21. nor discerning the *Baptisms* as
καθὼς ἔςιν
ἀλήθεια ἐν τῳ
Ἰησῦ. they are in their own *Nature*, and
in Spirit, or as the *truth is in
Jesus*.

The Baptists.

BAPTISM of Water being a
Legal *Ordinance*, though a
more clear administration of *Christ*,
was administered always by *persons* of more than ordinary *gift* and
spirit; for in all *Legal administrations* which pointed at and sha-
dowed *Christ*, still they were per-

formed by some properly, and spe-
cially, and extraordinarily enabled
for that *Office* or *Ministration*, and
therefore the *tribe* of *Levi* was for
administration of *Ordinances* then
under the *Law*, and *Abraham* for Gen. 17. 23.
circumcision, *Moses*, and *Aaron*,
&c. *John Baptist*, the *Apostles*,
and the more than ordinary gifted
Disciples, and *Philip*, and *Ananias :* nor is there any extant in
all the *New Testament* who did
administer *Baptism*, but they were
such as by a *power* and *gift* more
than ordinary could make *demonstration* of their calling to the administration of *water*, which was
first in that way of doctrine performed by him, than whom a
greater Prophet hath not risen,
even by *John* who Baptized; and
so *Philip* and *Ananias*, the one
working glorious miracles at *Sa-* Acts 8.
maria, the other having a *vision*
from God to warrant and glorify
his call to that *administration* upon
Paul, and so all the *Apostles*
and seventy *Disciples*, were such
who went about doing *miracles* as
men excellently gifted for *administration ;* and whereas the *Scrip-*

tures make mention of some *Disciples*, Acts 10. 48. as those with *Peter*, who did not appear to do any thing more than others; nor *Philip*, nor *Ananias* at the time of their *administration* of water; it ought to be sufficient to us, that the *Scriptures* doth set forth *John Baptist* and the *Apostles* and *Disciples* that were more than ordinarily gifted, and *Philip* and *Ananias* who had sufficient warrant to themselves by such glory upon them for that *Office* and administration of *water* upon any, and for those other *Disciples*, surely we see and read enough to tell us, in those that were so gifted; and in them and their gifts, there is *light* enough to shew us the *glory* of those *Baptists* that did undertake to administer, which in the *Scripture method* is sufficient for all others of whom the *Scripture* is silent.

And for that of *Christ's* Disciples, both in *John's* time and *Christ's*, and after his *Resurrection*, in the *Acts* of the *Apostles*, *baptizing* by *water*, we find this; That the Lord Jesus himself *baptized* none, but his *Disciples*, nor Mat. 10.

did he, in his first sending them forth, give them any power to *baptize* as in his *Ministery*, but they Baptized upon *John's* account, that of water being his ministration who *Baptized* unto *Christ* as well as they, though not in that clearness of *ministration* and *Doctrine*, as they did; and therefore *Paul* did tell the *Corinthians* he was not 1 Cor. 1. 17. *sent* to *Baptize*, and did it according to his spiritual liberty, he was a *Jew to the Jew, &c.* and *Peter* and the rest did it upon the like account: though I believe they were under more bondage to these outward things, as *washing*, for *Peter* was an *Apostle* to the Cir- Gal. 2: 8. cumcision, and *Ananias* who *baptized Paul* was a Jewish Disciple.

And further, I believe, that as the *Lord* did suffer the *Law* of *Ceremonies* to die out by degrees, and to be worn out by the *ministration* of the *Gospel*, so he did that part of *John's* Ministery, of washing, by the *Baptism* of Christ, of his *Spirit, I must decrease, but* John 3 30. *he must increase,* which surely was spoken not according to the *persons* of *John* and *Christ*, but according to their *ministration*, which is the great thing the *Scripture* takes notice on.

The Baptism of Sufferings.

THE *Baptism* of *Sufferings* is that Passion, *C*rucifying, and death, which the Body or flesh of Christ was to be Baptized or washed in; *Can ye be Baptized with the Baptism that I am Baptized with?*

τὸ βάπλισμα.
ἐγὼ βαπτιζο-
μαι. βαπλισθη
ναι.
Mat. 20. 22.

The Baptism of Sufferings is that in which the Lord Jesus was to be perfected according to the flesh; *it behoved him to make the Captain of our Salvation perfect through sufferings.*

Heb. 2. 10.
ἀρχηγὸν τῆς
σωτηρίας.

The *Baptism* of *Sufferings* is that Jordan; that stream or flood of Passions which all the Spiritual Israelites were to pass through; this was that River of Brimstone, which is kindled from the breath of the Lord Jesus himself, through the flowings of which he was able to conduct all his, and Land them safely upon the shore or land of Promise, or on the other side Jordan; *I have a Baptism to be bap-*

tized with, and how am I strait- Luke 12.
ened till it be accomplished! 50.
Βάπτισμα
This Baptism of sufferings is that βαπτισθῆναι.
in which all the whole flesh of
Christ is to be Baptized, all which
flesh is not that only which Christ
appeared in, but that of his body
or members, *With the baptism that* ἐγὼ βαπτίζο-
I am baptized with, shall ye be μαι. βαπτισ-
baptized, That I may fill up that θῆναι.
Mark 10.
which is behind of the afflictions .39.
of Christ in my flesh, for his Col. 1. 24.
τὰ ὑστερήματα
body's sake, which is the Church. τῶν θλιψίων
ἐν τῇ σαρκί.

The Baptism of Water or of John.

THE Baptism of water is *John's*
Ministery unto Christ: *I in-* Mat. 3. 11.
deed Baptize ye with water unto ἐν ὕδατι.
Repentance: the Baptism of water
was a Legal washing, and therefore
reckoned amongst things that are
Legal; *The first Tabernacle stood*
in meats and drinks, and divers Heb. 9. 10.
washings and carnal Ordinances,
which divers washings are called διαφόροις
Baptisms in the Greek. βαπτίσμοις.
The Baptism of Water was therefore in its Ministery administered
by *John*, who was a Prophet nearer

the more clear Revelation of Jesus
Christ than the rest, for a *greater*
Prophet than John *hath not risen,*
and therefore this Ministration was
administered by him who was a
Prophet, or one rather upon the
account of the Law than the Gos-
Mat. 11.11. pel, for *he that was least in the*
μικρότερος. *Kingdom of God is greater than*
μείζων. *he.*

The Baptism of Water was not
given in Christ's Ministery to his
Disciples or Apostles, who, when
he sent them out to preach first to
the Jews, gave them not one word
Mat. 10. 5. to Baptize; the Lord Jesus was
Baptized by *John*, the Minister of
Water, to fulfill righteousness for
his, the Righteousness of washing
which was Legal as Circumcision,
Col. 2. 11, therefore we are said to be Circum-
12. cised with him in Circumcision,
buried with him in Baptism; the
Baptism of Water was performed
by the Disciples and Apostles of
Christ in the Name of the Lord Jesus, as all other Legal Ordinances
were, for Circumcision and all was
to Christ, who was *the end of the*
Law; but Jesus Christ himself
never Baptized any, never was an

administrator of it in his own person, *he Baptized none, but his Dis-*
ciples, so as his Disciples Baptized
none, as his only Ministration, but
as from *John,* and as in his Ministration unto the Lord Jesus, and as
a Ministration which was begun by
one who was so eminent a Prophet,
and so acceptable to Disciples that
were weak and Legal.

John 4. 1, 2.

The Baptism of Water was more
used by those Apostles or Disciples
which were Jewish, and to the Jews,
as *Peter,* who had the Apostleship
of *Circumcision,* and so did Ju-
daize more; than by the Apostle
who was less a Jew, and had not
seen *Christ* in the flesh but in the
Spirit, and was an Apostle to the
Uncircumcision, and professed he
was not sent to *Baptize, but to*
Preach the Gospel.

Gal. 2. 8.
ἑις ἀποςολὴν
τῆς περιτομῆς.

1 Cor. 1. 17.
ȣ γὰρ ἀπέςει-
λε ἐμέ Χριςὸς
βαπλίζειν.

This Baptism of Water was called
a Baptism of Repentance, and of
Manifestation to *Israel,* because
that coming of *Christ* in the flesh
was the first opening of the Mystery of *Christ* in flesh *to those who*
were under sin and bondage, as
the Jews and the Gentiles were.

Acts 19. 4.
John 1. 31.

C

The Baptism of the Holy Ghost, or Gifts.

THE Baptism of the *Holy Ghost* or *Gifts*, is that Baptism which is said to be more properly *Christ's ministration, He shall baptize ye with the Holy Ghost and with fire.*

ἐν πνεύματι ἁγίῳ καὶ πυρί.

The Baptism of the Holy Ghost or Gifts was that Baptism which the Lord Jesus promised his Disciples to fulfil upon them, and upon their Ministration, *Go, teach and Baptize all Nations, in the Name of the Father, and of the Son, and of the Holy Ghost;* and *lo, I am with you, &c.* or, I Disciple those *Nations,* and Baptize them with the Holy Ghost in your ministration; for we all know that *Apostles* and *Disciples* could not disciple or *baptize* any: who is *Paul* or who is *Apollos?* and this Ministration of the Holy Ghost or Gifts was to last that Age, for so is the Greek, not *for* ever *and* ever, or to the end of the world, as is commonly read, but to the

Mat. 28. 19.

πάσας τὰς ἡμέρας ἕως τῆς συντελείας τῆ αἰῶνος.

Age, or during the time, or for the fulfilling of that ministration.

The Baptism of Gifts or the Holy Ghost was administered from Christ in the Disciples' ministration, *Be Baptized, and ye shall receive the gifts of the Holy Ghost; for the promise is to you and to your children, &c.* which *promise* is that of gifts or the *Holy Ghost*, which was that thing promised by *John* upon *Christ's* Ministery, *He shall Baptize with the Holy Ghost;* and was promised by Jesus Christ himself, *Ye shall* Acts 1. 5. *be Baptized with the Holy Ghost, &c.;* and *Paul laid his hands on* Acts 19. 6. *them, and they* received *the Holy Ghost;* and *the Holy Ghost fell on them,* this was a *promise* in the Joel 2. 28. Prophets too.

The Baptism of the Holy Ghost or Gifts and fire was in figure: Gifts held forth the flowing of a more spiritual Nature or of the Spirit upon those who were true spiritual Disciples, and fire was a sign or figure of the power of the Spirit in the spiritual Disciples, burning up and destroying flesh and the body of sin in them, even

this first *C*reation, upon which it
fell, for it sate upon each of them
in fire, signifying, by its resting
upon their flesh, what part was de-
signed to loss and purification;

1 Cor. 3.
13.
τὸ πῦρ δοκι-
μάσει ὡς διὰ
πυρὸς.

*The fire shall try every man's
work of what sort it is;* if any
man's work be burnt, he shall suffer loss, *but he himself shall be
saved, yet so as by fire.*

The Baptism of Christ.

THE Baptism of *C*hrist, which
is his own proper and Spiritual
and only ministration, is that by
which all true Christians are *Baptized* into *fellowship* with him, and
oneness with him; and so becomes
wholly washed in the New creature,
or New man, or Baptized into the
very *N*ame of the *Father, Son,
and Holy Ghost,* of which that
Baptism administered in gifts, or
the Holy Ghost by the Apostles,
more *visibly* was a sign.

εἰς τὸ ὄναμα
εἰς [into] τ῭
πατρὸς, &c.
2 Cor. 3.
17.
Col. 1. 15.

The Baptism of *Christ,* who is
the Lord that Spirit, the *Image
of the invisible God,* the quickening Spirit, is that one Baptism
spoken on in *Ephes.* 4, *One Lord,*

one faith, one Baptism, for Jesus
Christ administering in himself,
and his own Spiritual *Nature,* can
only make us thus *one* with himself, and with his own body.

The *Baptism of Christ* thus
Administered in his own *Spiritual
Nature* upon his, is that very Baptism by which we are in the fellowship of his sufferings and of his
*death: as many as are baptized
into Christ, are Baptized into his
death,* and *as many as are baptized into Christ have put on
Christ;* so as this Baptism, by
which we are all Baptized into
Christ, and put on Christ and his
death, is spiritual; for Christ cannot be truly put on, nor any thing
of his, his *sufferings, death,* or
resurrection, but in *Spirit* and
Truth, whereby we are truly *crucified* and *dead* with him, to ourselves and the world, and alive with
him in one spirit; *the same Spirit
that raised up Jesus Christ shall
also quicken our mortal bodies.*

The Baptism of Jesus Christ is
that whereby we are baptized into
his body; now his body is a *Spiritual* one, and fashioning like his

Eph. 4. 5.
ἓν βάπλισμα
[*unum*].

Phil. 3. 10.
Rom. 6. 8.

εἰς Χριστὸν.

Rom. 6.
Gal. 3. 27.

Χριστὸν ἐνε-
δύσασθε.
Christo in-
duti.

Gal. 5.
Rom. 8.
αὐτῶ πνεύ-
ματος.

1. Cor. 12.
13.
εἰς ἕν σῶμα
[*into.*]

Col. 2. 10.

τετληρόμε-
νοι.

Col. 2. 11,
12.

ἀχειροπόι-
ητοι.

Col. 2. 20,
21.

1. Pet. 3,
21.

glorious one, *by one Spirit we are all baptized into one body.*

The Baptism of *Christ* is that whereby we are complete in him; now we are complete in him only by being one with him in *Spirit* and *Nature: He being made unto us Righteousness and Sanctification, &c.* and thus we are said to be circumcised *with the circumcision made without hands, and buried with him in baptism, wherein also we are risen with him through faith,* or Spirit; so as we are Baptized in him as we are *Circumcised* in him, that is, we are all in him; and as the Circumcision is without hands, so is the Baptism, it being the Apostle's whole business in this Chapter to take us and the *Colossians* up higher than rudiments, which perish with using.

The Baptism of Christ is that true spiritual *washing* and *cleansing* wherein all his are *baptized,* not the putting *away the filth of the flesh, but the answer of a good Conscience towards God by the resurrection of Jesus Christ,* and this is the Baptism which is said in this place to save us, as *Noah's* Ark did those eight persons in figure, therefore saith the Apostle, *the like figure whereunto Baptism doth now save us.*

ἡμας σώζει.
1 Pet. 3. 20.
Βάπτισμα ἡμᾶς σώ- ζει ἀντί- τυπον.
Exemplar.

The Divers Ministery, with the Ministery of Christ in his Saints.

UNDER the Law there was a Priesthood, the administration of the Law and Sacrifices being gathered up into one Tribe, that of *Levi;* none was to take this office *but he that was called of God, as was Aaron.*

Heb.

Under the Law there were Prophets, as *Moses, Samuel, Elijah, Isaiah, Ezekiel, &c.* the Interpretation of the Law, and the more spiritual Revelation of the Will of God, were administered by the Prophets, or some few to whom the Word of the Lord came.

Both Priests and Prophets were Types and Figures of Jesus Christ to come, the great high Priest and Prophet of his people as well as in ministry to the people.

Heb.

In the more clear Revelation of the Gospel, the administration of Christ was committed to a few, or certain Disciples in distinction of Gifts and Office; twelve of whom Mat. 10. were called Apostles, and seventy Disciples.

When Jesus Christ went out of *flesh* into *spirit*, or ascended, he confirmed and settled this *ministration* by pouring out gifts of *Spirit* for the more glorious and visible quickening and spiritualizing this Ministration; he ascended up on high *and gave gifts unto men*, he gave some Apostles, some Evangelists, some Prophets, some Pastors, some Teachers for the work of the Ministery, &c.

Eph. 4

During the Ministration of Jesus Christ in the Church in this distinction and diversity of gifts, there were such as were spiritually and visibly gifted accordingly, so as the Apostles and Evangelists, and Prophets and Pastors were known to be such, both by the Saints or people of God, to whom they did according to their gifts administer, and to themselves, they administering in the knowledge of such gifts of Spirit as were in them.

1. Cor. 12, 10.

1 Cor. 9.

During this Ministration of Jesus Christ by Apostles, Evangelists, Prophets, Pastors, &c. the Disciples that were not in the distinction or number of such, but were only called Disciples, yet did Preach and administer as they had received. Acts 8. 4. Rom. 12,6.

' Antichrist, or the Mystery of Iniquity, came in upon this Ministration by gifts and Ordinances, and the glory of the Spirit and power of gifts went off from the visible Church, as the glory of God from the Temple to the threshold, till it was wholly departed; this was the *falling away* prophesied on by *Paul,* and by *John* in his *Epistles,* and in the *Revelation,* in the vision of the *Churches of Asia,* and of the Beast, and false Prophet. 2 Thes. 2,3. 1 John 4. 1, 3. Rev. 2. 3. chapters. Rev. 13.

All things in the visible Churches of the Nations were, and are, in the absence of the Spirit and of gifts, administered by Arts and Sciences, and Grammatical knowledge of tongues and languages, and according to some spiritual measure received in some, to whom these things are in some degree *sanctified and spiritualized.*

All knowledge and understanding

of the Original, all Interpretation of Scriptures is according to the outward and inward administration of both, through Arts, Sciences, and tongues acquired, and through such a measure of spiritual understanding as each have received.

There is no restoration of these gifts of Spirit, which were in the first ministration of the Church, as of Apostles, Evangelists, Prophets, Pastors, Teachers, according to the first institution, that is, so as the gifts of all these Offices are clearly to be seen and discerned in Spirit, to be the very *unction* and *gift* either of Prophet, or Pastor, or Teacher, as in the first Ministration, which will more clearly appear in singling that pure gift of Spirit that is in each from the habits of Arts and Sciences, and Languages acquired; and from that Spiritual understanding which is in all the Saints, according to that work of the Spirit, or regenerate part in them, which is one and the same for nature and substance of *regeneration* with all; so as no superadded, or proper, or distinguishing gifts appear upon any other account, but either a *natural*, or *arti-ficial*, or purely *Spiritual* account; not upon any account of distinction of *gifts* and *Office* as at first, when the Spirit was poured out, and this will appear yet more in comparing *times*, and *persons*, and *gifts;* our *times* with the first, our Pastors even of all *Churches* with the first, and the *gifts* of all now with the *gifts* then: then the *Spirit of God* was poured out in *gifts*, and the Disciples were *taught* of *God*, and *Prophesied* and *Preached* from the mere *gift* and *spirit* received; but now *Prophets* and *Pastors* are taught from another account, *viz.* upon a more *Artificial* and *in-dustrious*, and *humane* account, and their *regenerate Nature;* then they ministered and spake as the *Oracles of God*, then they spake as the *Spirit only gave them ut-terance.*

The Ministery that is raised up Acts 2. to destroy *Antichrist*, or the *man of sin*, which prevailed against the first *ministery* and *gifts*, is to be more glorious, and powerful, and mighty, as the *Ministery* of *gifts* was more excellent than that of the *Law;* and so destroyed that power of *Apostacy* that had prevailed upon the *Priesthood* and *Law* then; so the Ministery that is to destroy that *mystery of iniquity,* which prevailed upon the Gospel *Ministery of gifts,* must be more excellent, and glorious, and powerful than that, and this is *Jesus Christ himself, called the* Acts 3. *Prophet whom we are to hear;* Heb. 8. and that GOD, of whom *we shall all be taught; Ye shall be all taught of God;* and he that shall destroy *Antichrist by the brightness of his* coming, and that *An-* Rev. 14. 6. *gel* with the *everlasting Gospel,* Rev. 18 1. prophesied on by *John, preaching and enlightening the earth with his glory;* this is *the day of Jesus Christ,* whose coming *is* Hos. 6. 3. *prepared as the morning.*

The Ministery of *Jesus Christ,* Rev. 18. 1. this *Angel of the Covenant,* is through his people, who are his *Angel,* or the *Angel* and *Messenger* to him, as he is the *Angel* to God or *Messenger,* or *he* that was *sent of God;* and this Ministery is a Ministery of *Jesus Christ* in *all his Saints* or *people,* according to his administration of *light*, and *glory*, and *truth* in them, shining in them to the revelation of *truth* and the *Gospel*: This Ministery exceeds the *Priesthood* of the law, which was but in one *tribe*, and one *sort* of men, and was but a Ministery of *Christ* to come in the *flesh;* this Ministery is of *Jesus Christ* the *Prophet* in the *whole body* of his Saints, come in the *flesh*, and *perfected in spirit*, and *entered into glory.* Luke 24.

The Ministery of *Jesus Christ* the great Prophet in all his *saints*, or *people*, or body, is a Ministery exceeding the Ministery of the *Gospel* in *gifts of miracles* and *other gifts;* for *that* was in some, *this* in all, that of *men* more immediately, this of *Jesus Christ* more immediately; that of some *gifts*, which, though excellent in their *nature* and *operations* of the same *Spirit*, yet these might be such as were not *spiritual*, but *carnal;* but the pure Ministery of *Jesus Christ* in his Saints, in himself, as he is the *quickening Spirit* and *Lord from heaven*, is in none but such as are of his *body* and in one *Spirit* with him.

The present *Ministery* of men
amongst all the Churches at this
day according to any appearance
of the *Spirit of God* in them,
though running through the *chan-
nel* of *Arts, Sciences,* and *Languages* acquired by *natural* power
and *industry,* is such a *Ministery*
as we may hear and receive or partake of anything of *God* or *Christ*
there, that we find in their *administration,* though this be not that
pure *Ministery* of *Christ in Spirit,*
as we find the *Apostles* and *Disciples* of *Christ* in the *Jewish worship* in the *Synagogues* and *Temple* under the *Apostacy* and *Cor-
ruption.*

Zeph. 2.   And this *Principle* of *bodily*
and *local separation* I find is both
Legal, and *Jewish,* and *literal;*
1 Cor. 8. 4, and is sucked in by the *Saints*
5, 6.   from the first Gospel discoveries,
and from the *law,* and *Mosaical*
principles of *separation,* and when
the Spirit of God is more in them,
they shall see it, and hath been, as
I clearly find, no little hinderance,
and is at this day, to the *power* of
the *Gospel,* and *Jesus Christ* in
Spirit, and the *body of Christ* in

the *unity of the Spirit;* and since our controversies in these outward things and *Churchways, &c.* have increased, the *law of love* and *Spirit,* and *power of godliness* hath much abated; while *form* and mere *letter,* and something of *outward order,* have taken up the place.

And though this may be an *offence* to such, as *Paul* saith, who *make* conscience *of the Idol;* yet *we know,* saith he, an *Idol is no-* thing, nor an *Idol Temple;* but when they shall see the *Christian* as he is in *Spirit,* and the *new Creation,* and no other thing part of him but what is *glory, spirit,* and *life,* and that all the *law* of *outward* order and *form* is only a supplement to the *absence* of the *Spirit* of God, and to order their *outward man* amongst *men* to their *fellow saints* and the *world,* while the law of the *Spirit of life* is not in them *shining,* and *conforming* them in *Spirit* and *love* to the *Image* of *Christ.* And for my part I am far from denying any Gospel *form,* or way which appears to be the practice of the *Saints* then, because I conceive that *saints* see

1 Cor. 8. 4, 5, 6.

gathering and *practising* are yet under such a *ministration*, and are to walk in it while they are in *bondage* and *weakness*.

But, on the contrary, I am far from thinking these administrations to be our *glory* and high point of Reformation, which our *Brethren* of the *Independent*, and *Baptism*, and *Presbyterian* way do, but in all tenderness, love, and yet faithfulness to them, rather a *ministration* of *bondage* and *weakness* to the *Saints*, because the Scriptures make it clear, calling such *ministrations* our *seeing darkly as in a glass*, and *seeing in part*, and *that when the more perfect is* come, *then that which is in part shall be done away.*

1 Cor. 13. 8, 9, 10, 11, 12.

The Passage from lower Ministrations to higher.

THE administrations in which God hath appeared, and doth appear yet in some proportion, are these:

1.   The *law* or *righteousness* of the

first *Creation*, in which *God* had communion with *man*, and *man* with *God*, yet rather as with a *Creator* than with a *Father* or an *Immanuel*, and in the outward *Court*, or first *Creation*, not in the *inward* or *holiest; Paradise* itself being but an *Image* of the *excellency* of this *Creation*. Gen. 1. 26. Gen. 2. 7, 8.

Gen. 2. 15, 16, 17, 18.

Man having fallen through the *temptation* of the *serpent*, or *fleshly wisdom*, and the espousals of the *woman*, or the *weakness* of that *Creation* wherein he was made, hath the first *law* of *righteousness* presented to him in a new ministration of *letter* by *Moses* in *Tables* of *stone* from *God*, in which the first *glory* and *excellency* was ministered to man in his *fallen* and *apostated* condition. 2. Gen. 3. Exod. 20. 2 Cor. 3. 7.

And because the *law* or first *righteousness* was *weak* through the *flesh*, there was the lowest ministration of *Angels*, viz. by *vision*, *dreams*, &c. added, and likewise a ministration of *Priests*, *Sacrifices*, *Ceremonies*, *Tabernacle*, *Temple*, *Prophets*, by which *man* might have access unto *God* and speak with him, yet but in the *outward Court*, Heb. 1. 1.

or *flesh*, or *things* of this *Creation*, though be filled these with another *glory*, a richer and a more *excellent* discovery of his *love*, in the promised seed.

There was another *ministration* Exod. added, of *war* and *peace* of the *Nations*, enemies in the *flesh*, and of Josh. a *promised land*, or *blessing* in the *flesh*, and the *Israelites* or *Jews* were to pass under this *ministration*, through all the *enmity*, oppositions, and battles of the *Nations* to this *Canaan*, all which was accomplished to them in *letter*, and in that in figure of a more spiritual enmity, and *kingdom*, and glory, which is fulfilled in the more *Gospel-revelation*, when the *fulness of* time came.

The next *ministration* is something clearer than all these, and something *brighter* than the *law*, yet not so *clear* nor full as that of the *fulness of time* which followed it, or of *Christ* in the *flesh*, and this *ministration* was that of *John*, Mat. than whom a greater *Prophet* did not rise, yet he *that was least in the kingdom of God was greater than he ;* he was *a burning and a shining light.* The *law and the prophets were till John,* he was the Prophet of the Highest, and was sent to prepare his way, and to make *Christ manifest to Israel* by *word* and *water,* and this was only a *ministration* in order to one more *spiritual,* was to *decrease,* as the other did *increase :* the *Baptism* of the *Spirit* or fire was to lick up this of water, as in that *figure* of the *sacrifice* performed by *Elijah* the Prophet, when the fire came down and sucked up all the *four barrels of water.* John. Luke 1. John 1. 31. John 3. 30. 1 Kings 18. 34 to 38.

The other Ministration was the *Gospel* in the *flesh* of *Christ,* or in *gifts* and *ordinances* something more clear and in more *discovery,* and *revelation;* for the *flesh* of *Christ* in which he *taught,* and did *miracles,* and was *circumcised* and *baptized,* was a copy or draught of that *ministration of gifts* and *ordinances,* which was as perfect as the first *Creation* in its *glory* and *purity,* and yet *higher* and *nearer* to God, coming forth in more *revelation* of an *Immanuel,* or God with us. Mat.1. *cap.* 3. *c.* 4.

A further Ministration was more

nearness and participation of God manifested in *flesh*, or of *Christ;* and that was in *graces* or *operations* and *fruits* of the *Spirit*, as Gal. 5. 22. of *faith, repentance, love, self-denial, humiliation, meekness*, all which are a sweet spiritual administration, even the light of *the* 2 Cor. 4. 6. *glorious Gospel of God shining in the face of Jesus Christ.*

Another *Ministration* respectively to a more excellent *glory* to come, is that by *Angels* in their *highest* administration, which is the only *Angelical* and *Seraphical revelation*, being something below the *Spirit*, yet *higher* than *reason*, or man's highest principle; and this *John* received all those more excellent *discoveries* to be fulfilled in Rev. *chap.* 1 and 2. their seasons.

There is another Ministration of more *Spirit*, of *love, meekness, self-denial*, suffering, overcoming *evil* with *good*, and conquering by receiving in the *wrath* and *enmity* of the world; and this I take one of the last and glorious *truths*, respectively to the *flesh* and the world, into which God will gather up his people by times and degrees, from all *worldly* and *fleshly* interests and engagements, wherein they shall be carried up into a more full enjoyment of *God*, and conformity to *Christ* in his *sufferings, death,* Phil. 3. and re*surrection.*

' The Lord Jesus walked first in this truth, he was led as a sheep to the slaughter, *when he was re-* 1 Pet. 2. *viled, reviled not again, when he* 23. *suffered he threatened not.*

The Lord Jesus revealed this Gospel-truth, and distinguished it from the *law,* which *law was, an eye for an eye, and a tooth for a tooth.*

But he saith, re*sist not evil,* but whosoever shall *smite thee on the* Mat. 5. 39. *one cheek turn to him the other also.*

Ye have heard it hath been said thou shalt love thy neighbour, but I say unto ye, love your enemies, *bless them that curse you, do good* Mat. 5 41. *to them that despitefully use you and persecute you,* that *ye may be the children of your heavenly Father.*

The *Apostle* to the *Romans* reveals this; dearly beloved, *avenge not yourselves, vengeance is mine, &c.*

Rom.   If *thine enemy hunger feed him, if he thirst give him drink;* for in so doing thou shalt heap coals of fire upon his head.

Be not overcome *of evil, but overcome evil with good.*

The Lord Jesus *prophesied* of

Mat. 5. this, *blessed are the meek, for they shall inherit the earth;* through their meekness they shall inherit, through their meekness only shall the *jealousy* and *enmity* of the Nations be allayed concerning them.

John in his vision of the latter times saw an appearance of this.

Rev. 14.   Here *is the patience and faith of the Saints, of them that have the commandments and the faith of Jesus;* to which that of the *Apostle* to the *Hebrews* answers, *there remaineth therefore a rest to the people of God, and he that is entered into his rest hath ceased*

Heb. 4. *from his works as God did from his.*

The last, and more *full*, and rich *Ministration*, and most *naked*, is that of *God* by *himself* in *Spirit* to the *sons* of *God*, into which *Jesus Christ the forerunner is* Heb. *entered,* and *I saw no Temple therein,* for *the Lord God Al-* Rev. 21. 22, 23. *mighty and the Lamb are the Temple of it.*

And this *Ministration* is fulfilled then, when *Christ shall have delivered up the kingdom unto God;* and this is not only done upon the *whole body* of *Christ* at the last, but is fulfilled in its particular *accomplishments,* and mystery of *Spirit* here, there being found these *transitions, passages,* and resignations, and exchanges of glory in the Saint.

He that can receive *it let him* receive *it.*

The more full and naked Ministration of *God* by himself in *Spirit,* and *I saw no Temple therein, for* Rev. 21. 22, 23. *the Lord God Almighty and the Lamb are the Temple of it.*

And as God hath appeared in all these former, saving the last, into which Jesus Christ hath entered, so they remain still as *figures* and as so many several Signs or Planets in *this Creation* and the *other,* for believers to be *born* in,

and to pass through in some *pro-*
portion and *measure* till *C*hrist
1 Cor. 15. hath *delivered up the kingdom*
unto God.

God hath appeared in all these
former *administrations* to his *peo-*
ple, and they have enjoyed him in
these *degrees,* and *distances,* and
approaches; and they remain still
as *figures,* and as so many signs
and planets in the first *Creation*
and the *second* for *Christians,* in
some *measure* and proportion to
pass through; so as he that is of
any *spiritual* discerning in these,
may be able to *comprehend* with
all *saints* what is the *height,* and
depth, and *breadth,* of God's *mi-*
nistration to his People, and to
know *Saints* according to the measures they receive, and the *minis-*
tration they live in with *God.*

I have drawn out these ministrations in their particular or*bs,*
and *sp*heres, and circles, which I
could have folded up in three only,
of *Law, Gospel,* and *Spirit,* or of
letter, graces, and *God,* or of the
first, second, and *third heavens;*
but I saw *God* something *abound-*
ing and variously *dispensing,* and

I followed him in that *fulness* and *variety* so far, as he hath lighted my candle.

I shall now discourse a little more generally of all these, and of the passage from these, and of *God* appearing in these, and his *going out* from these, till he hath *scattered* all these *veils* before him, that *he* and *his* may see and enjoy each other with *open face, where we shall see as we are seen, and know as we are known.*

The *Christian* passes through several *ages* and *dispensations;* as *Christ* was in the world, so is every *Christian;* he was made under the *Law,* under *Circumcision,* under *Baptism,* and the *Supper of bread and wine,* and then he crucified all that *flesh* he walked in under those *dispensations,* and entered into *glory,* for thus it *behoved Christ to suffer and enter* Luke 24. *into his glory.*

The Jewish Church, or dispensation which was according to *Moses,* and the *letter* in which they were led out in carnal and more fleshly courses, as in the proceeding against the *Nations* by *war* and *fighting,*

D

with all their other legal *rites* and *rudiments*, were a clear figure of the *C*hristian under age, or under *tutors and governors*, and worldly *rudiments*.

The Disciples of *C*hrist, according to *John's ministery* and *Christ's* in the *flesh*, were another type or figure for all Disciples of their *age* and *ministery*, and the *S*pirit of *C*hrist works in all the *Disciples* according to such way, and proportion, and measure, and dispen-

Gal. 4. 1. sation, *the heir as long as he is a child differing nothing from a servant, though he be Lord of all, until the time appointed of the Father.*

And I could not speak *unto*

1 Cor. 3. *you as unto spiritual, but as unto*
1, 2. *carnal, even as unto babes in Christ, I have fed you with milk,* and not with meat.

And the great and excellent design or mind of God in all these things, is only to lead out his *peo-*

Rom. 1. *ple*, *Church*, or *Disciples* from
2 Cor. 3. age to age, from *faith to faith*,
18. from *glory* to *glory*, from *letter* to *letter*, from *ordinance* to *ordi-*

nance, from *flesh* to *flesh,* and so
to *Spirit,* and so to *more Spirit,*
and at length into *all Spirit,* when
the Son shall deliver up the kingdom unto the Father, and *God
shall be all in all,* which last
transition, or *resignation,* or *reso-
lution* of all into the *kingdom of
God* is not, as some think, only
when the fulness of times or ages
is come, but is transacting and
finishing in *parts* and *members* of
the body of Christ, and is not one
single act, point, or effusion of
glory, but a perfecting and ful-
fulling it in the several members
of Jesus Christ, till the *fulness of
the stature of Christ* be made up,
and *the Church become the fulness of him that filleth all in all.*

For *the day dawns, and the* 2 Pet. 1.
day-star arises in the heart, shin- 19.
ing more *and more unto a perfect
day ;* and he who is the *bright* Rev. 22.
and morning Star, is still shining
into the glory of *the Sun of righteousness,* and the *light of the
Moon* shall become *as the light of* Isa.
*the sun, and the light of the Sun
as the light of seven days,* till

the Lord God himself be *the everlasting light*, and *our God our
Glory*.

Thus is the *Christian*, or *Disciple* of Christ, passing on upon
the several degrees and measures
into the *glory* of *Christ*, and *crucifying* each condition as he passes
through it, as all the Disciples have
done before: the Jews passed out
of that of the *Tabernacle* into the
Temple, and from thence into the
flesh of Christ, that *Temple destroyed and raised up in three
days*, a greater than *Solomon* being
there, and from thence into *Christ
Crucified*, and so into a *ministery*
of *spirit* and *life*.

And the *Disciples* all of them
had a measure of time and season
in each Ministration, and God had
his when he filled the *Tabernacle*
with a *cloud*, and the *Temple* with
Glory, and the *flesh* of *Christ*
with *unction* or *spirit* above his fel-
lows; and while God lived in each
ministration, quickening, and *glo-
rifying*, and *acting* it for himself,
that presence of God and of Spirit
was to the Disciples like the Sun
in Summer shining upon them, *the*

candle of the Lord shining upon Job 29. 3, 4. *their heads, and his secret upon their Tabernacles.* But when the line of God's season was run out to its *point* and *extremity*, that he would no longer stay there, nor have his glory inhabit in such or such a *ministration*, then that *ministration* became but a place of *desolation*, a solitary *place for the Satyrs to dwell in, and the* screech *Owl to sing in*, that is, for the *Spirit* of *Apostacy* and of *Antichrist* or iniquity to possess and act in.

And for *Disciples* to stay longer in any *ministration* than the *Lord* or the *life* and *Spirit of Christ* is in it, is as if *Lot* should tarry in *Sodom, Israel* with the *Ark* when God was departed, the *Jews* in the *Temple* when the *Veil* was rent, and the *glory* gone off to the *threshold*, and from thence too ; their *house* being left unto them desolate, even that *house* or *ministration* where the *light of God* did formerly dwell.

As if the Disciples of *Christ* that went into the Grave should step in and sojourn there where his *body*

had lain, and was risen and gone,
seeking the dead amongst the living.   The disciples of *C*hrist were
a true figure of such who, when
*C*hrist was dead, were *embalming*
the *body*, and would preserve it
with *spices* and oi*ntments* when the
spirit and *life* was out of it.

The *Jews* were a figure of such
who would preserve their *Law*, and
the *shadows* of all their worship,
when *C*hrist had left them, who
was the *life* and *substance* of all
Mat. 26. 51,
52. that *ministration.*   *P*eter and the
rest were a true image of such, who
in that *sword* he wore was a true
figure of all such as *Christ* suffers
in a *warlike* and *defensive* posture
about his flesh, or whom he suffers
to be so far conformed to the
fashion of the world, as to guard
and preserve those *fleshly* privi-
leges of his *presence* and power
amongst them, and in that activity
of his to rescue and preserve that
flesh and body in which so much
glory and *excellency* had appeared,
and so many *miracles* were done,
beyond that point or end of *ministration*, which *God* even the *Father* and the Son himself had set,

was a figure of all such as should
stretch out any dispensation or ministration of God farther than the
line or *spiritual* sinew of it will
bear.

The Spirit and Life of Out-
ward Ordinances.

THE second *Man* or *Adam*, in
whom we all live, is a *quickening Spirit*, and the *Lord from
heaven*, and is at the *right hand
of God, viz.* in the *choicest glory*
of the *Father*.

That by which the people of God,
or all true *Christians* are born, is
the seed of *God*, or *Word of God*,
or the *divine nature* of *Jesus Christ*,
or the *Spirit of God*, which is
called *snnctification*, regeneration.

That the true spiritual Christian
is that *new creature*, that sanctified *one*, or *regenerate one*, who
is thus born, and hath *Christ formed*
on him, and this new *creature* is
fed by the *Spiritual* life of Christ.

That the *new creature*, or *spiritual man*, is one who receives all
his *growth* and *increasings* in the

power, *seed,* and *Principle* of the
Spirit of God, or *Jesus Christ.*

That the *Ministery* or Ministration by which he grows up to that
fulness of *stature* in *Jesus Christ,*
is a *Ministery* or *ministration* of
glory and *spirit.*

That the true and *spiritual Baptism,* by which every *Christian* is
baptized into *Christ's death,* is the
Baptism of *Blood,* which is the
righteousness, spirit, or *life* of
Christ.

That the due and spiritual *Sa-
crament* of the *Lord's Supper* is
the very *body* and *blood* of *Christ*
in the *Spirit,* or that pure *spiritual
nature* of *Jesus Christ, quickening*
and *feeding* up the *Christian* into
a *spiritual life* and *union* with
God.

That the true spiritual *Minister*
is *Jesus Christ,* who is called a
Minister of the *Sanctuary* which
the Lord *pitched and not men.*

That *Jesus Christ* is the true
Spiritual Apostle, sent out from
God to reveal the Father, and is
so called by the *Spirit* of God in
Scriptures, the *Apostle* and *High
Priest* of our profession.

That *Jesus Christ* is the true spiritual *Prophet* that teaches his people, so as they are all *taught of God*, and is so called in *Scriptures* a *Prophet, which the Lord God raised up instead of Moses.*

That the true *Spiritual Pastor* is *Jesus Christ,* who is that one *Shepherd* prophesied on, who can lead his people only into *green Pastures,* or places of life.

That the *Spirits* of just men made perfect, or the true *C*hristian in spirit, are those true spiritual *Elders* in the *New Testament.*

That the true *Church* of *Christ* is that spiritual company whom Christ hath washed in his blood, clothed in his *righteousness,* sanctified in his spirit, *espoused* to himself; this is the *City of the living God,* the *heavenly Jerusalem,* the *general Assembly* and *Church* of the *first-born,* the *House,* and *Temple,* and *Kingdom of God.*

That the true *spiritual keys* of the *Kingdom* of God is the very *Spirit* of God, the very Spiritual power of Jesus Christ upon *believers* and *unbelievers,* who hath the *keys* of *David,* and *opens, and no man shuts, and shuts, and no man opens.*

That true *spiritual excommunication* is Jesus Christ, who is mighty in *Spirit* and *Power* in all his, pronouncing an *anathema maranatha* or curse upon *all flesh*, and delivering the *body* or sinful *flesh* over to *Satan*, or the *power of darkness*, whereby *flesh* and every fleshly member is cast out from all *communion* with God and Jesus Christ, and from those who are indeed *born of God*, and are the true *Spiritual Church* of God, which is no more than that true difference and distinction which Jesus Christ puts betwixt the *precious* and the *vile.*

The true Spiritual Gospel-Order, which the *Apostle* rejoiced to behold, is that *spiritual distinction* and variety in the *body of Christ*, wherein one Member differs from another in *measure of Spirit*, and *Glory*, and *Power*, and yet all *complete*, and make perfect that *body* of Christ in the Spirit; for he being a *spiritual head*, must have a *spiritual body.*

The true *Spiritual government*

is Christ reigning in the Saints in Spirit, ordering them in thought, word, and deed, holding forth his *power*, and sceptre, which is a *sceptre of righteousness* against *flesh* and *blood, Principalities and Powers, spiritual wickedness* in high places.

The true *Spiritual Covenant* is the *New Covenant*, which God makes with us in *Christ*, and wherein he is manifested to be their *God*, and they his people, to teach them, and *write his law in their hearts.* Heb 8.

The true *Spiritual Ordination* is the hand of Jesus Christ, stretched out or laid on upon the *Spirits* of such Christians as preach or *Prophesy* of the *Ministery* of the *Gospel*, that is, such are rightly and purely or*dained* and *sent out*, who are sent out from the *power* of the Lord Jesus, to *whom all power in heaven and earth is given*, and are *anointed* of him to preach the Gospel, and *sent* of him, who *ascended* to give *gifts unto men*, some *Apostles*, some *Evangelists*, some *Prophets*, some *Pastors*, some *teachers*.

The true spiritual *trial* or exa-

mination of the *gifts* of any is then,
when the *Spirit* of the *Prophets* is
only subject to the *Prophets*, that
is, when the gift by which any one
speaks of *Jesus Christ* is manifested in the *hearts* and *spirits* of
the *Saints* when they see the truths
they minister as they are in Jesus,
and in themselves, and in them that
are spiritual, and truly *anointed* by
the same Spirit; and so are all
Prophets according to the *measure*
given, or as they are all *baptized
into one spirit* and *body*, and have
all received of his *fulness*, who is
that great Prophet raised up of our
brethren like unto *Moses*, and are
redeemed to be *Kings*, and *Priests*,
and *Prophets*, even partakers of
all his *offices* in Spirit, he being
the spiritual *head* of all his, who
are the spiritual *body*, his *Church*.

The Christian under Episcopacy, Prelacy, Presbytery, Baptism, Independency, &c..

THE whole world was divided into *Jew* and *Gentile ;* the Jew was that only *visible Church of God, to whom pertained the glory, and the adoption, and the Covenants :* and yet this *Jewish Church* was exceedingly fallen from its *glory* and *purity* both of *Priesthood,* and *Worship,* and *Administrations,* when Christ came : So as now the *Prophecy* seemed to be *fulfilled,* they were now *without a King, and without a Priest, and without a Sacrifice, and an Ephod, and a Seraphim ;* and were corrupted with many *traditions* and *doctrines* of men, *teaching for doctrines the traditions of men :* Thus was the *Jew,* and their *Church.* Hosea.

The *Gentile* had changed the truth of God into a lie, and *had worshipped the creature more than the Creator ;* and had changed the glory of the incorruptible God, and Rom. 1.

were given up to a reprobate mind,
and were therefore called *sinners* of
the *Gentiles* alienated from *the life
of God, strangers to the Covenants
of* Promise; thus were the *Gentiles* full of Idols and Idol temples,
sacrificing to *devils,* and that way
of the *knowledge of God,* which
was both in the *law* written in their
hearts *accusing* or *excusing,* and
in the whole *C*reation, where the
*eternal Power and Godhead was
clearly seen,* even in the things
that did appear, even that way of
the knowledge of God in them was
darkened, and *they became vain in
their imagination,* and *their foolish
hearts were darkened.*

Now when *Jew* and *Gentile* were
both thus, yet God had his people
amongst both, amongst the *Jew,*
where *Zacharias* the Priest, *Elizabeth,* and *Mary,* and *Joseph,* and
Simeon, and *Nicodemus,* a Ruler
of the *Pharisees,* and *Joseph* of
Arimathea, with many such, were
like so many *Stars* in a dark night.

Among the *Gentile* there was a
Job, a Queen of *Sheba,* a *woman*
of *Canaan,* the *wise men* that came
to *Jerusalem,* the *Greeks* that came

to see *Jesus, Cornelius* the Centurion, so as in every *Nation he that serveth God, and worketh righteousness, is accepted of him,* Acts 10. 34. *and God is no respecter of persons.*

When *John* came, who *was a burning and a shining light,* he preached to, and baptized all *Judea,* who went out to the Baptism of *John,* and taught his Disciples by forms of Prayer, and such *rudiments,* to their weakness, and God had his people here that were under no more knowledge of Christ, nor higher revelation, than this washing to Repentance, and to him that should come after him, and this low way of *communion with God* in forms or rules of *Prayer* given out by *John,* for so *John taught his Disciples.*

When *Christ* came preaching the *Gospel of the kingdom,* and teaching in Parables and Mysteries, he had a People and Disciples who knew little of his sufferings, that he should die and rise again, as *Peter,* and the rest, and knew little of that glorious doctrine and *truth* which he spake and preached to them, till he took them alone and expounded to them those *Myste-ries ;* and his Disciples were under a form and *rule of Prayer* as *John's* were ; *Lord, teach us to pray as John taught his Disciples:* They saw little more of him than his *fleshly presence* and *miracles,* they loved him, and clave to him, and followed him, but had very *few discoveries* of him in Spirit, except some few of them, *James,* and *Peter,* and *John,* before whom he was transfigured in the Mount, which was but figurative and typical of a more *spiritual revelation ;* And when the Spirit of *Christ* was come, and the Apostles were sent forth in clearer evidences and de-monstrations of *Truth,* then some were under *John's* Baptism, and knew not of any *Holy Ghost ;*

Rom. 2. 23. some were under the *law,* and zea-lous of the Law and *Circumcision;* some regarded a *day,* some eat *herbs,* some were *eating* such

1 Cor. 8. things as were *sacrificed* to *Idols.*

So as here God's people were found, some in a corrupted Church, as that of the *Jews,* some under *false worship* and *traditions,* some under *Legal* rites, under *forms* or *rules* of *prayer*, some under *John's Baptism*, under *bondage* of *days* and *times* and other *outward things*, under the ignorance of *Christ's death* and resurrection, and of the *holy Ghost*.

So as all these things considered, there will spring these *Conclusions*.

That the *Nations* commonly called *Christians*, who are under the account of others as false in their Church-*constitution, worship, forms, and order*, yet these things are not exclusive to the true *Christian* in *Spirit*, or one *born* of God, but in these commonly called *Christians*, though under *Episcopacy*, or *Prelacy*, or *Presbytery*, yet there may be such as have the true *seed of God* in them, partakers of *Jesus Christ*, true *Disciples* of *Jesus Christ*, respectively to regeneration or the *new birth*, if they wait in the *increasings* of *Christ*, Rom. 1. and revelation of *righteousness* 17. from *faith* to *faith*.

That there are true and *spiritual Disciples of Jesus Christ*, under *forms* of *Prayer*, who have little more communion with God than in those *forms*, as of *Common-*

Prayer, Book-prayers, outward *rules* of worship; so as they wait in these to come up into higher *revelations* of *Spirit* when discovered to them.

That there are such who are *Christians* anointed by the *Spirit* of *God*, under observations of days, times, *meats*, *drinks*, several opinions of *Christ*, of the *Holy Ghost*, of the *resurrection*, of *Church* order, of *Baptism* of *Water*, which is *John's* Baptism, called *Anabaptists*; so as they all in these several measures pass on·from *faith* to *faith*, and *glory* to *glory*.

Rom. 1.17.
2 Cor. 3.
18.

The Christian in Truth.

THAT which forms, essentiates, or constitutes the true *Christian*, is the *Spirit of* Jesus Christ, *that which is born of the Spirit is spirit*, so as a man is a *Christian* from *birth*, as he is born a *man*, so he is born a *Christian*, both are from birth, and *seed*, the one of *flesh*, the other of *Spirit*.

The *Christian* is one who is of

the *second Adam*, as all men are of the *first*, and the second man is the *quickening spirit*, the Lord from heaven, and so are they that are heavenly.

The Christian is one in whom *Christ is formed* or figured, (as the Greek word implies) one that bears the *image of the heavenly man;* who is the *Image* of *Jesus Christ*, as Jesus Christ is the Image of the invisible God.

The Christian is one who hath the incorruptible seed in him, or *the word which liveth and abideth for* ever, which *word* is the Lord Jesus Christ, who quickens the Saint, and is the life of the Saint, *you hath he quickened who were dead in trespasses and sins.* Eph. 2. 1.

The Christian is one who is in *fellowship* and *conformity* with *Jesus Christ* in his *crucifyings, death,* and *resurrection,* in whom the *flesh,* and *life* of the *flesh* must die, as it did in him, and the Christian, as Christ did, must live in *Spirit* to God.

The Christian is one who is the *new creature,* or *new man,* for he *that sits upon the Throne* in his *Spirit* saith, behold I make all

2 Cor. 5. 17.

things, all new, *old things* in him, as corruptions and lusts, do pass away.

The Ministery that hath been since Antichrist or the Mystery of Iniquity reigned without, or in the Worship of God in all Societies of Christians called Churches, whether in Presbytery, Independency, or Baptism, is not the same with that first Ministery of the Gospel in pure gifts, and is no other than the Witnesses in Sackcloth.

Eph. 4. 8.
ἀναβὰς εἰς;
ὕψος; ἔδωκε
δόματα.
Eph. 4.

THE Lord Jesus *ascended* up on *high*, out of flesh into *Spirit*, and gave *gifts unto men*, he gave some *Apostles, some Evangelists, some Prophets, some Pastors, some Teachers.*

In this *administration* of *gifts*, the *mystery* of Jesus Christ, or the Gospel, was revealed and carried on till the time *Prophesied* on by the Spirit of God, wherein the *mystery* of *iniquity* should prevail, and the *falling away* should be, and the *man* of *sin* should be *revealed*, and *perilous times* should come: and this *mystery of iniquity* did so darken and overcast all this administration of the *Gospel* in *gifts*, and or*dinances*, or *outward administrations*, as there was a visible *Apostacy* respectively to those very pure *gifts* of the *Spirit*, and pure administrations respectively to the first *institution*, and this is no more than the experience of our own age, and the times before, so far as any *History* can make apparent, doth clearly demonstrate; so as that administration of *Spirit* or *Ordinances*, which hath been in several times since the first pure Gospel-day, or *time* (wherein the Spirit did minister in *truth* and *demonstration*) hath been but in some faint and small discoveries of the *Spirit* and *Letter*, as in those of *Huss, Luther, Wickliff, Calvin,* Peter *Martyr*, and *Bede*, with all the rest of our many Martyrs in the *kingdom*, who were glorious *lights* respectively to the darkness of that generation, yet if compared

2 Thes. 2.
2 Tim. 3.
ἔλθῃ ἡ ἀποσ-
τασία πρῶτον
καιροὶ χαλε-
ποὶ.

with the pure glory of the first
Gospel-administration in *gifts* and
or*dinances*, were far below, and in
darkness and *weakness* to that; so
as I look upon all God's ways of
the *administration* of his *Gospel*
to hold some *proportion* one with
another; the *Tabernacle*, and *Temple*, and *Laws* of outward *administration* were in such ways and
means *God* did appear in; and so
in the *Priests* and *Prophets*, God

Hebr. l. l.
πολυμ**ε**ρῶς
καὶπολυτρὸ-
πω

at *sundry times and in divers
manners*, speaking to our *fathers*,
and afterward *God* took up our very
flesh to administer in, and so came,
and spoke to us by his *Son*, and
after all these, the *Lord* went out
from these after his *usage* of them,
and appearance in them, and then
they were no more an or*dinance*
or *way* to *God*, as they formerly
were; nor did ever the *Lord* enjoin
the *restitution* or *reassuming* of
them again, when the *Temple* was
once rent, the *veil* of it, the *Lord*
was no more in it, nor in their
Priesthood and *Sacrifices*, &c. nor
when once the *Lord Jesus* had
ended his *administration* in the
flesh upon the *Cross*, did he ever

restore it in that very way again, or intend it according to that first appearance, but in a more *glorified* state.

And so in all *reformations* respectively to these former *administrations*, they never returned back, or reassumed the same again, after once God had refused it, and laid it by. When *Christ* came in the *flesh*, he did not make it his work to settle the *Priesthood* again, but to lead them into the *spiritual glory* and fulfilling of all those *legal* dispensations, and carry them on into more *Gospel*-administrations, and that which was more *excellent* and *perfect.*

So it is in that first *Gospel*-administration of *gifts* and *ordinances* after *Christ* ascended, there were such pure *operations* of Spirit, as in *gifts*, and some outward *institutions*, and *Church-administrations*, but these were only the *Ministration* for that *age*, as the *Tabernacle* was for its age, and the *Temple*, *Priesthood*, and *Sacrifices* for their age, and the *flesh* of *Christ* for its age or time; so as the *falling away* is no more, but the *Lord gathering* up, or *taking* in the out-goings, *operations*, or *gifts* of his *Spirit* in such a way of *ministration*, and till this was done, there was a *withholding* of the *mystery* of *iniquity* from being revealed; therefore saith the *Apostle* to the *Saints*, Ye know what *withholdeth that he might be revealed in his time*, and *he who letteth will. let, till he be taken out of the way;* and truly that *mystery* did not work freely, nor powerfully, till the *Lord had* removed the *glory* of his Spirit from the *Churches*, the presence of which did exceedingly prevent, and *withhold*, and put an hindrance to the *revelation* and *dominion of that man of sin.*

And the Spirit of God foreseeing *God* about to leave this *ministration* of Gospel-*glory* to the world, and bring a *night* upon all that *day* and *brightness* of his *Son*, prophesied of the *times* to come, and to succeed that *glory, viz.* in the *last days perilous times* shall come, men shall be *lovers* of themselves, *covetous*, proud, *boasters, &c. despisers of those that are good,*

2 Thes. 2. 6.
τὸ κατέχον.
v. 7.
ὁ κατέχων.

2 Tim. 3. 2—5.

high-minded, lovers of pleasures more than *lovers* of God, having *a form of godliness,* but denying the *Power* thereof.

But there were false *Prophets* among the *People,* even as there shall be *false Teachers* amongst you; who *privily shall bring* in damnable *Heresies, &c.* and many *shall follow their* pernicious *ways, by reason of whom the way of truth shall be* evil *spoken of,* and through covetousness shall they make *merchandize of you.* 2 Pet. 2. 1, 2, 3.

Beloved, remember ye the *words which were spoken* before of the Apostles *of our Lord Jesus Christ,* how *that they told you there should be mockers in the last times,* these be they, *Separating themselves,* having not the *Spirit.* Jude 19.

Little *children, it is the last time, and as ye have heard that Antichrist should* come, *even now are* there many Antichrists, *whereby we know that it is the last time.* 1 John 2. 18.

So as from all these places of the *Apostles,* we may see their *Prophesies* of the *Antichristian* times, which are the *times* of the

E

flesh, and of the *Spirit* of *in-iquity*, reigning amongst the *Saints*, or in the *Christian* world, the *Lord* of *Glory*, *Jesus* Christ in *Spirit*, being all this time cru-cified in *Spiritual Sodom*, *Egypt*, or *Babylon*, which is the *Kingdom* of the *Flesh* and the *Powers* of *Darkness*, and this is the State and condition of the *Church* of *Christ*, or those who are the *Spi-ritual vessels*, or *Golden* cups of the Lord's *Temple* *and* carried away captive, and live under the *Power* of *Flesh*, and of *Spiritual wickednesses*. So as all the time of the reign and *Prevailing* of this *mystery*, (which mystery is in a threefold *Principality* or *emi-nency*, viz. of the beast, the *false Prophet*, and the *devil*, all which *three* work as well without, unto the world, as within, in the *flesh* of every *Saint*,) all the time of this reign or prevailing is not a time of any *restitution* or *restoration* of the first *ministery*, or *gifts*, or *or-dinances*, as was in the *Apostles'* times, but is the state and perse-cution of the *Lord Jesus* in *Spirit*, and the time of the *woman's* being

Rev. 19, 20.
τὸ θηρίον με-τὰ τᾶτε ὁ ψευδοπρο-φήτης ὁ διά-βολος.

in the *wilderness*, all *things* in this
time seeming as a *waste* and *barren*
dispensation about her, not inha-
bited by the *Spirit* of *God*, and she
in a retirement of *Spirit* dwelling
with *God*, out of the power of the
Dragon, who casts only his *flood*
after her, but not upon her.

So as here is no more in this
time of *Antichrist's* reign in the
Flesh and the *World*, but only the
Church's oppression in *Spirit*, and
the *crucifying* the Lord in *Spirit:*

And all these appearances of the
Lord Jesus in many glorious *Saints*
who in particular ages appeared
were but *appearances* of him who
is that *Faithful* and *true witness*,
against this power of the *man of
sin*, and were but *drops* of the
vials, *Soundings* of the *Trumpets*,
openings of the *Seals*, before the
Battle of the great *Day*, when *fire*
shall come *down from God* out of
heaven and devour them, the *Lord
Jesus* being revealed in flames of
Spirit, and *glory*, against all *Flesh*.

So as there is not any *word* appearing in all the *Scripture*, that
the first *ministery* by *gifts* and
ordinances shall in any measure be

Rev. 12. 6.
ἡ γυνὴ ἔφυ-
γεν εἰς τὴν ἔρη-
μον.

Rev. 20. 9.

continued, though in part, or in
reservation to be restored, as if
this were the great work the *Lord*
intended to bring to pass, *viz.* the
setting up a purer *ministery* of
gifts to teach his *people*, or restoring some *legal* ordinances, as
Baptism of water, the *church* way,
or *Presbytery* of *Elders*, and all
the *glory* of the last times or ages
should be only the bringing in these,
and taking them out of the hands
of *Antichrist*, all which arise from
a mistake of the *type* of the *Jewish
Apostacy* and *captivity* which
figured out the *Spiritual* Church
or new *Jerusalem* in *Babylon*, or
Captivity to the *flesh*, or *man of
sin* in all his deceivableness and
Power, and the restoring of all
shall be only the appearance of the
Lord Jesus, who shall destroy *Antichrist* with the brightness of his
2 Thes. 2. coming, and the *two edged Sword
of* his *mouth*, his *Spirit*.

And there is not a word spoken
in all the *Scriptures* of these things
to be restored, as *gifts* and ordinances, but the *glory* of the *Lord*
in *Spirit*, and therefore the Reformation or Restoration that the *Lord*

Jesus brings with him, (for *Moses,
Joshua,* and all the reforming
Kings of *Judah,* were but types of
him, the *last* and most excellent
and glorious Reformer, *King* of
Kings, and *Lord* of *Lords,*) that
Reformation, I say, that he brings
with him, is the *revelation* of himself in *Spirit, he* and *his Father*
being the *light* and *Temple* of his
people, for there shall be no other
there.

Rev. 21.
22.
Isa. 60. 19.
ναὸν ὀκ εἶδον
ἐν αὐτῆ ὁ θεὸς
ὁ παντοκρά-
τηρ.

This shall be a glory without
Sun, or *Moon,* or *Stars,* or any
such low or faint appearance as
gift or *ordinance,* but the *Lord
God shall be* the *everlasting light,*
and *God the glory;* and light
shall cover *the earth as the waters*
cover *the sea:* light shall not
Sparkle or be in bright beams as
in *a gift* or an *ordinance,* but it
shall flow out from the Lord himself, even cover the *earth,* swallow-
ing up or overflowing all earthly
administrations. And it shall be
as much *Apostacy* in the *Saints*
to go back to that first ministery
of the *Gospel-times,* which was the
ministery to the first *discovery* of
that *mystery* hid from ages, as it

would have been in them to have gone back to Jewish Temple and *Priesthood*, &c. And have taken the setting up of those to have been the great and only *Reformation* of *Christ* come in the *flesh*, and as the *Lord Jesus* himself did in his coming in the *flesh* fulfill all these, and destroy nothing, save only as to the *outward* and perishing *nature* of those ordinances and *Rudiments* of the law : So in this his *last glory* to be revealed in the *saints* here, he shall not destroy any of the first ministery of the *Gospel* by *gifts* and or*dinances*, but shall fulfill it; it being but a *type* of his *glory* to be revealed in the *Saints*, and the former ministery is only destroyed as to that outward *Perishing* part of it.

And this destruction of *Antichrist*, and the *glory* to be revealed, is the *Prophecy* of the *Prophets*, and *John* in the *Revelation*, and is the sum and substance of all *types* and *ministrations* which were before.

So as all the pretended *Reformations* by *gifts* and *Ordinances*, which tend to a reducing us to that

first *ministery* of the *Apostles'*
times, which that of *Presbytery*,
of *Independency*, and *Baptism-
way* endeavours, is but a building
up such things as the *Lord* would
have destroyed; it being an administration which he would use no
longer, and therefore suffered *Antichrist* to prevail upon it, and the
man of sin to overcome it, and as
God to sit in the Temple, or in all
that outward *form* and *worship*,
figured out in that word the *Temple* as *God*, or as *God* himself used
to do, when he was pleased to appear there.

And therefore all that *ministery*
and *Pastorship* and teaching is not
at all upon the account of the first
Gospel *ministration*, according to
that very *glory* of the *gifts*, and
pure *anointing*, by which they did
minister as the oracles of *God* and
very *truths* of *God*, as they did
then, so far as they *Spake* or did
any thing in the *Holy Ghost:* but
they now, I mean the *Pastors* and
ministers, do Speak and *minister
doubtfully, darkly, uncertainly,*
more in the *flesh* than the *Spirit*,
not at all in any thing of unction

or *anointing* exceeding any private *Christian*, or distinct according to any *gift* of the *Holy Ghost*, but so far only as they exceed others in parts, wit, or learning, which are upon a lower account of the *Spirit* than the first *gifts* upon that of *Arts* and *sciences*.

And therefore if *Pastors, ministers*, and *Christians*, who cannot now minister as the or*acles of God*, nor according to the very *gifts* of the *Holy Ghost* then, will be content to *Prophesy*, as *Christ* Rev. 11. will only allow his *Witnesses* to do, even all that bear *Witness* of *him*, in *Sackcloth*, according to that *poor, low*, and *legal* account and humble condition they are in, it being yet the *time of Antichrist's* reign, not of *Christ's*, and not assume to themselves the *names, Offices, Pre-eminence, glory, obedience*, very *administrations*, which were then in *power* and in the *Holy Ghost*, both in *Pastor* and *Churches*, Rev. 3. and not walk as *full*, and *rich*, and *wanting nothing*, when as they are *poor, miserable*, and *naked*. The Rev. 3. *Church* of *Laodicea* being a *figure* of all such, for my part, I then shall look on all such as in the *Spirit*, and walking humbly with God, and *prophesying* in *sackcloth*, and waiting for the coming of the *Lord Jesus;* nor do deny but Christians in these *ways and administrations* have enjoyed God sweetly, though they be not such ways as God approves on, though he suffer: as many of the Godly *Bishops* and *Martyrs* did enjoy *Jesus Christ* in their times of *Ceremonies* and *Forms of Prayer*, God still appearing to his, as they are in Christ, not in such or such an outward way or form.

There remaineth two or three choice Scriptures to open concerning this, and they are these:

And he gave some Apostles, and some Prophets, and some Evangelists, and some Pastors, and some Teachers, for the perfecting of the Saints, for the work of the Ministery, for the edifying of the body of Christ, till we all come in the unity of the faith, &c. Eph. 4. 11, 12, 13.

And God hath set some in the Church, first Apostles, secondarily Prophets, thirdly Teachers; after that, miracles, then gifts of 1 Cor. 12. 28.

E 2

healing, helps, governments, diversities of tongues.

Mat. 28   Go ye therefore and teach all Nations, *Baptizing them in the Name of the Father, and of the Son, and of the Holy Ghost.*

Teaching them to observe all things whatsoever I have commanded you, and lo I am with you to the end of the world.

From all these Scriptures these Conclusions are made:

1. That there is a Ministery of gifts, of teaching, and ordinances.

2. That this is for the perfecting of the Saints.

3. That this is to last to the end of the world.

Now these Scriptures are much mistaken according to such results and conclusions.

The Scripture to the Ephesians, *Eph.* 4, shews only that there was such a Ministery of *gifts and offices*, but not any such continuance of them to the *end of the world*. For where it is said, for the *perfecting of the Saints, &c. till we all come, &c.* that hath relation to the tenth *verse*, or to *Christ ascended*, that he might *fill all*

πρὸς τὸν καταρτισμὸν τῶν ἁγίων.

things; and this of the *perfecting of the Saints, &c.* is only an exposition or clearer interpretation of that tenth *verse,* how he *fills all things,* viz. by *perfecting* his *Saints* in the *work* of the *Ministery,* or that glorious and spiritual administration of himself upon his, to bring them all into the *unity* of the *faith,* so as he may be *one* in *them* and *they* in *him,* the *Lord* one, and *his name one,* which is that *unity* of the *faith.*

*N*or can this Scripture intend any other thing than this, *viz.* to shew first how the Lord *fills all things,* as in verse the *tenth,* and how he set up a *ministration of gifts* in the first discovery of *Gospel glory,* he gave *some Apostles;* and how he himself *perfects* the *saints* by being their *fulness,* and so *edifies* or *builds* up his *body,* and brings forth that *unity* of the *faith,* or one glorious *evidence* and *revelation* of himself in the whole *body.*

*N*or can any other thing bear the weight of such expressions but Christ himself. Who can *perfect* the *Saints* but *Christ?* Who can

μεχρὶ καταντήσωμεν ἐι πάντες.

ἵνα πληρώσῃ τὰ πάντα.

εἰς ἑνότητα τῆς πίστεως.

edify the *body* or build it up but *Christ?* Who can bring forth unity of *faith* but *Christ?* For no *gifts* either of *Apostle* or *Prophet,* or *&c.* can *perfect the saints.*

1 Cor. 13. 2, 3. Though I have the gift of *Prophecy,* and *understand all mysteries,* and all *knowledge,* and though I have all *faith,* and have not *love,* or Christ, who *is the love of the Father, it profiteth me nothing.*

But suppose it were so, that the Ministration of *gifts* and *offices,* there spoken on, were for the *perfecting* of the *saints* till the *unity* of the *faith* be, what doth this prove to the present Ministration of *gifts* and *offices* now, or since the *falling away* amongst us, for we have none of them in the pure *gifts* of the *Holy Ghost* or *Unction,* and we must either have all or none; there is no taking these *gifts* and *offices* in *pieces* and *parts,* as they do generally, distinguishing them into *extraordinary* and *ordinary;* the *extraordinary,* they say, are *Apostles, Evangelists, Prophets,* and these, they say, are ceased; but *Pastors* and *Teachers,* they say, are *ordinary,* and remain. But where is this distinction to be found in the *Word?* are not all *gifts* of the same *Spirit?* Doth not the Scripture reckon them all equally necessary in the *Church?* Doth it any where speak of *Apostles, Evangelists, Prophets,* only for the first Age, and *Pastors* and *Teachers* for the Ages after? Doth not the Scripture say expressly, he hath set some in his Church? 1 *Cor.* 12. 28, and so reckons according to some order in the *excellency* of *gifts* and *office,* not according to the expiration of some, and the life and continuance of the rest, saying, *Apostles, Evangelists, Prophets* are to cease, only *Pastors* and *Teachers* remain; but he saith plainly he hath *set* all these in his *Church,* not excepting one sort more than *another;* nay, a *Pastor* or *Teacher,* in the *true* and proper *gift* and *office* was as *spiritual* as the other, *viz.* of the *pure anointing* or the *Holy Ghost;* but Pastor and Teacher hath been considered in a lower capacity, and *industry, art, natural parts,* and *learning* have been taken in in after times to the composition of a

ἔθετο ὁ θεὸς ἐν τῇ εκκλη- σία.

Pastor and *Teacher*, and upon this account those *offices* have been thought or*dinary*, which were upon the mere and pure account of the *Holy Ghost:* so as if they will have Pastors and Teachers only remain, where is the Scripture for excepting the rest, and where are the very same *gifts?* And pure *anointing* of *Spirit* for *watching, feeding,* and *teaching?*

And if they will have these Scriptures to hold forth such a continued *Ministery* of necessity to the perfecting of the *Saints,* where are all the rest, *viz. Apostles, Evangelists, &c.* for all are reckoned both in *Eph.* 4, 1 *Cor.* 12. 28, and where are those very *gifts* of pure *anointing?* And why so many hundred *years* without these? What hath become of the *Saints* since the first great *falling away?* How have they been *perfected?* If all these were for that very *work,* and yet not *visibly* extant for so many years? Nay, the pure gifts of the *anointing* of the *Holy Ghost* not appearing in any of the most glorious *Reformers,* as *Luther,* who had much darkness, as in that of *Consubstantiation*, and in his passions to King *Henry*, and in many other particulars of his, &c. and so of the rest, save only they *shone* forth in the more *glory* because of the *darkness* of that *Generation*.

For that other Scripture in *Matthew* 28 : Go, *teach* and *baptize*, and *lo I am with you*, it is only (as I take it) and merely in application to the Apostles and Disciples of that *Age* and *Ministration* whom the *Lord* bid *go* and *teach* what he had *commanded* them, and *baptize* into the *name* or *mystery* of *God*, which word *baptize* is a *figure* *C*hrist uses to express the *depth* of a spiritual *mystery*, as in that, can ye *be baptized with the Baptism that I am baptized with?* And be shall *baptize you with the Holy Ghost, &c.* And that phrase, to *the end of the world*, is (if more clearly translated) to the *finishing of the Age*, or that *Age* of *Ministration*. πάσας τὰς ἡμέρας ἕως τῆς συντελείας τῦ αἰῶνος.

Some of these things are scatteringly spoken on in other places of my Book, but here more perfectly and clearly.

Magistracy a Power or-dained of God.

THE Magistrate is a power *or-dained of God*, an *Image* of the *Power* and *Judgment* committed to *C*hrist; Scripture and the gift of *wisdom, justice,* and *righteousness* are his *unction* now, as the oil or *anointing* was his *unction* under the Old Testament.

Rom. 13

Magistracy for *form* is not one and the same, but divers, according to the several *polity* of *Nations* and *Kingdoms,* by *Kings* singly, or *Kings* and *States* jointly; as in this Kingdom, or *States* singly, as in the old notions of *Monarchy, Aristocracy, Democracy,* and that each *Nation* is subject according to its polity and form to the respective government, and that Scriptures clothe and invest that form in its very first *being* and *constitution,* and that *form* receives an *Image of God* upon it, as the first *man,* who as soon as he became such a model of *earth* or *clay* became a *man,* and had the glory of

God upon him, and *dominion* over the creatures.

These *Powers* and *Magistrates* upon earth are set up for the punishment of *evil doers*, and for *the praise of them that do well, jus-* Rom. 13. *tice* and *righteousness* being that very *line* or *golden* reed by which they are measured, the very *Scales* by which God *weighs* them, *where if they be found too light, he* Dan. 5. *gives their Kingdoms to another.*

All lawful subjection is to be rendered, *honour to whom honour,* Rom. 13. *tribute to whom tribute*, and *subjection to every ordinance of man for the Lord's sake; Prayers and Supplications* are to be made for them, that *we may lead a peaceable and a quiet life in all godliness and honesty.*

Magistracy is set up, not only to be an *Image* of *Christ* to the *world*, but to administer Peace and Judgment to the world and *Societies* of *men*, and more principally to his *people* in the *flesh*, who while they are *nursing fathers* to them do administer truly, and to Christ in his *people ;* when *Persecutors*, Christ still turns their *administra-*

tion, though evil in itself, into good
Rom.3. 28. for *his, all things working toge-
ther for good to those that love
God.*

The high and glorious design of
Christ in Magistracy is to open a
way in all their kingdoms and do-
minions for the *Spirit of God* to
breathe in, *Kings shall be thy fathers, &c.* and walk in, in such outward administrations as it pleaseth
the Spirit of God to appear in to
the Saints, who are in flesh and
weakness, and so far as concerns
any outward administration of
Christ, *Jesus Christ* becomes a
subject in his *Saints* to the *power*
he hath committed to *Magistracy,*
they having power to hinder and
further his spiritual *design* so far
as it comes forth in the outward
man; therefore all power of Magistracy turned against the *Spirit of
God* in this appearance shall, and
all such Kingdoms and *Nations* as
proceed accordingly, *viz.* to oppose
that Kingdom, Power, and Dominion they receive from Christ
against him in his spiritual Kingdom, shall be dashed to pieces like
a potter's vessel, *Be wise now*

therefore, O ye Kings, and be in- Psalm 2.
structed, ye Judges of the earth.

But all such Nations, States, and Kingdoms as shall administer not only judgment and righteousness in the world, but shall bring their *glory* and *honour* to Christ and his Rev. 21.
Spirit in his People, *Peace* shall ²⁴. be within their walls, and *prosperity* within their *Palaces, judgment shall flow there like a river, and righteousness like a mighty stream.*

The discerning of Spirits.

THERE was such a *Manifes-tation* of *Spirit* given to the people of God in the first *Gospel-times* as they could in the very *unction* or *anointing* of God *discern* Spirits and *try Spirits, Ye have* 1 John. 4. *an unction and ye know all things,* the *same anointing teacheth ye,* 1 Cor. 12. to another *the gift of discerning* Spirits.

In this Manifestation of *Spirit* were all *False-teachers, Deceivers,* 1 John 4, *Antichrists,* and *Hypocrites* judged ₂ John 7. and discerned; I will *come to you,* 1 Cor. 4. *saith the Apostle, and will know,* 19.

*not the words of them that are
puffed up, but the power.*

This *Manifestation of Spirit* is
that in which Spiritual men are
known and revealed to each other,
and have as full assurance of each
other in Spirit and in Truth as *men*
know *men* by the *voice, features,
complexions, statures* of the outward man.

The *Manifestation* of Spirit may
be darkened and clouded in Christians sometimes, and hath been in
the purest times, when the Disci-
Acts 8. ples did not know *Simon Magus*,
nor *Demas*, nor *Hymenæus*, and
Philetus, nor those that went out
1 John, 2. from them, nor *Judas*.
19.

    The Manifestation of Spirit hath
been much lost and darkened in
the Churches for many *hundred
years,* since the *Antichristian darkness* was upon them ; and therefore
they have judged Spiritual things
in a mist, and in much *dimness* and
doubtfulness, it hath been neither
night nor day.

    For supplement of this *Manifes-
tation of Spirit,* Christians walked
by *Candle-light* and *Star-light*,
and set up marks and signs of trial

and demonstration in the letter and outward man, so as any hypocrite might appear for a true *Christian;* and therefore most of their way of *Manifestation* hath been from formal *relations* and confessions of faith, and experiences according to the *Law* or *standard* of their own Spirits, trying and judging all other measures of grace by their own.

The experience of Christians, who have the *Spirit* of God in them, is very clear concerning the workings and *manifestations* of the same *Spirit* in others, as in *Prayer, Preaching, Prophesying, Conference, Conformity* to Christ, *Spiritual* conversation, so as Christians can in a manner say, the *Spirit* of God is here and here, or here I taste and see *something* of *God;* here is a *spiritual* savour, there is none ; as in natural things there is such a proportion betwixt the *sense* and *object,* that the sense knows and discerns its own object, as in *smelling, tasting, seeing, hearing,* so in *Spirituals;* and as there is an *outward,* a *letter,* or *Scripture-Christianity,* by which men are distinguished as *Jew* and

Gentile, as *Professors* and *Profane,* as of the visible *Church* and of the *world,* so there is in the true *spiritual* Church, or *Kingdom* of *God* in *Truth,* a more pure spiritual and glorious way of knowing each other according to that true spiritual *glory, nature,* and *light* Eph. 5. 8. that each walks in, being all *children of the day* and of the *light.* And this is no more than the fulfilling of that promise, then *shall ye return and discern between the righteous and the wicked, between him that serveth God and him that serveth him not;* but it is in that *day* when the Lord *makes up his jewels,* which is the more glorious *revelation* of *Jesus Christ* in the *Saints,* gathering his people into more *unity* and *glory* of *Spirit.*

All *works* and *fruits* of men, as they are *Christians* and *spiritual,* must either be *judged* and *discerned* in the same *Spirit* and *measure* of *light* and *glory* in which they are *wrought,* and from whence they flow, or else it is but a mere *formal, outward, pretended, false,* and fleshly way of *judging* in those that so *judge;* and thus the tree is truly and purely known by its *fruits,* and *faith* by *works:* The same *Faith* and *Spirit* shining and discerning, in those that judge the works of their faith, who are judged.

And thus we may see how *Synods,* and *Councils* of men, and *visible* Churches have erred in their *judgments* and *discernings* of all others, judging all higher attainments of *light* and *glory, heresy and schism;* and by this sentencing the Lord himself, and confining him only to their own *measures* and *degrees,* which is that very *spirit* of *Antichrist* sitting in the *Temple* of *God,* and judging as *God,* nay, judging *God* himself according to his other *manifestations* which they see not, nor receive, unless they pretend to be that only *select Apostleship* for *interpretation* and *revelation* of Scripture, as the *Apostles,* who were the first *Preachers* of Scripture; and this they must do upon their *ways* and *grounds* of *discerning;* but what shall be done to these that *judge* before the *time,* and the *day,* or more full *revelation* of Jesus *Christ,*

the *false Prophet* shall be taken
and cast into the *lake that burns
with fire;* and these that judge
God in their *brethren* according to
such manifestations as are not in
themselves, shall be judged of *God*
their *Judge,* even of the *Lord Jesus,* the *Judge* of *quick and dead:*
Cain was an *image* of all such,
judging his *brother's sacrifice,* and
for that was sentenced of God.

Principles of War and Peace.

Βασιλεία ἐπὶ βασιλείαν. ἔθνος ἐπὶ ἔθνος. πολέμως; ἀκοὰς πολέμων.

1. **W**AR is the more natural
work of the *Nations* of
the *World,* who shall, according to
Christ's Prophecy, be dashing one
another in pieces till the last appearance of *Jesus Christ,* there

Mat. 24. 6, 7. shall be *Wars* and *rumours of
Wars, Nation shall* rise *against
Nation, and Kingdom against
Kingdom.*

2. War is from the *Law* and
Principles of *nature,* according to
which the *Nations* of the *world*
live and are acted, having no *higher
a law* to raise them, and *carry*

them up into more *glorious dis-pensations ;* For the *Law* or *Prin-ciples* of *nature* dictate thus, *pre-serve thyself,* thy *life,* thy *lands,* thy *rights,* an eye *for an eye, and a tooth for a tooth.*

Exod. 21. 24.

3. The true *Christian,* so far as he is in *nature,* and under this *law,* he is *acted* according to the *world,* and to the mere *Principles* of *na-ture* and *law ;* and therefore it is that the *Christians* to this day are found at the same *work* with the *world,* and *two are grinding at one mill,* two are in *one field,* two in *one bed ;* that is, the true *Chris-tian* and the mere *natural* man are together in one *work,* at one *plough,* in one *bed* or *way* of *Peace* and worldly *rest,* till the *Lord Jesus* be more manifested in *Spirit,* or in his *coming* and *revelation,* and the *one,* or *true Christian,* be *taken,* and the other *left,* the one taken up higher into more Spirit, and more of Christ, the other left in their mere nature, and *legal* prin-ciples, and worldly doings.

Mat. 24 40, 41.
δύο ἐν τῷ
ἀγρῷ δύο ἐν
τῷ μύλωνι.

μία πάρα-
λαμβανεται,
μία ἀφίεται.

4. The *Jews* were not only a *type* of the *true spiritual Church,* but of the *Christians* under the

F

lowest dispensation; and in the *model* of their armed *Tribes* and *Generals,* as of *Moses* and *Joshua,* were a figure of the *C*hristian un- der *pupilage* and *bondage* to *na- ture,* and the *laws* of *nature;* and so they were led out against the *Nations,* who were a *figure* of *worldly Tyranny* and *oppression,* to recover their *land* of *rest,* or such worldly privileges as they had in *promise* and *donation* from God.

5. Under the *Gospel* the Lord suffered the same *figure* in *Peter,* who walked about with *Christ* in his *fleshly* appearance, with his sword girt about him, and attended his *Person* till *Christ* bid him *put it up again* into his *sheath,* because he was now going out of that dis- pensation of *flesh* into more *glory,* into the same *glory* that he had with *God* before the world was, and was accordingly providing a more *spiritual dispensation* for them, even the *Comforter* or *Spi- rit of truth,* all which were a figure of all the Disciples of *Peter's fel- lowship* and *weakness,* whom the Lord would suffer in an *armed* and *defensive Posture,* till he provided

Marginal notes:

Exod. 13. Josh. 1.

Gal. 4. 2.

ὑπὸ ἐπιτρόπυς καὶ οἰκονόμες.

Mat. 26. 52.

ἀπόςρεψον σȣ τὴν μά- χαιραν εἰς τὸν τόπον αὐτῆς.

John 17. 5. Luke 24. 26.

εἰς τὴν δόξαν αὐτȣ.

a more *spiritual Ministration* for them, and a way of more *spirit*, *light* and *glory.*

In order to Peace, and Suf-fering, and Love.

I.

The Will *of* God.

A CHRISTIAN is most *per-fected* in the *Will* of God, in laying himself down to *rest* in the *bosom* of such *providence* as the *Lord* opens to him ; for nothing creates *perplexity* and *disquietness* of *Spirit*, but when the *will* of *man* is in *complying* and in a *motion* distinct from the *will* of *God,* when the Spirit of *man* moves in its own fleshly *course* and *circuit*, and so runs out into a *dispensation* further than the *law* of present *providence* will fairly allow it: and in this way men study, *plot, desire, lust,* are *passionate, inordinate, un-quiet, unstable,* and like the *trou-bled sea, foam* out themselves ; upon this account, men *lust* and

James 4. 2.
ἐπι θυμεῖτε
ὐκ ἔχετε.

have not, they *kill* and *desire* to have, and cannot *obtain*, they *fight* and war, yet they *have not;* are

Isa. 26. 17.

with child, and bring forth *wind*, and work no *deliverance;* they say the *bricks* are fallen down, but we will *build with hewn stones;* the *Sycamores* are cut down, but we will *change* them into *Cedars.* The *Lord* Jesus held forth another *pat-*

Heb. 10. 7.
τὸ θέλημα
σᾶ.

tern and *figure*, Lo, I come to do *thy will*, O God; not *my will*,

John 4. 34.

but *thine* be *done;* it is my *meat* and *drink* to *do the will of my Father;* the *Apostle* answers this,

Phil. 4. 11,
12.
αὐτάρκης
εἴναι.

as in *water* face answers face, *I have learned in whatsoever state I am, therewith to be content;* I can be *abased*, and I can *abound:*

1 John 4.

the reason of all is, from the spiritual *anointing* they receive, by

Eph. 1. 18.
πεφωτισμέ-
νυς ὀφθαλ-
μὸς.

which their *understandings* are *enlightened* to see all the various *workings* and contrary *contextures* of *providence* meeting in one *point*

Rom. 8. 28.
παντὰ συνερ-
γεῖ ἐις ἀγα-
θὸν.

or *line*, the *will* of God; so as all things *work together for good* to those that *love* God.

2.

God changing Dispensations.

THE Christian is most at *peace* 2. when he is willing to be gathered up by *God* from such *ways* . and *ministrations* below as he hath lived in formerly, if he see God clearly in it, for *God* hath his times of *letting* out, and *winding* up, of using such or such a ministration, and then breaking it, and laying it by, and appearing in other, and we must not *limit the Holy One of Israel*, nor fix him always upon the same *point* of dispensation, he went out from his *Tabernacle* into his *Temple*, from thence into the *flesh* of *Christ,* and so into *ordinances*, and *gifts*, and *graces*, and *Spirit;* with the *Jews* he was in *war*, in *peace*, in *captivity*, in *deliverance*, or return; and in this exchange of dispensation, *God* reveals and shines forth his *wisdom*, *glory*, and *power* upon *his* and upon the *world*, which wisdom,

power, and glory being in that fulness and infiniteness in himself, cannot appear in one *globe* and *ball* of
glory below, upon this *Creation,*
but as in *parts,* and *scattered
beams,* and *divers* workings; and
therefore *John* saw the *Lord in a
vision* like a *Jasper* upon *a Throne,
and a rainbow round about the*
Throne; which *rainbow* is a *glory*
of many colours, or a *figure* of the
glory of *Jesus Christ* in many appearances of things below.

Rev. 4. 3.
ἶρις κύκλοθεν
τȣ θρονȣ.

3.

The Law of Nature and Grace.

THE Christian is one who
should live in an higher region
than *flesh,* or *nature,* and when
God saith *come up hither,* he shall
live there, even in *Spirit* with him;
so as though *grace* destroys not
nature, yet it *perfects* and *glorifies* nature, and leads it out into
higher and more excellent attainments, than it can find in itself;
nature lives by this *law.* Preserve

thyself, thy *life,* thy *lands,* thy *rights* and *privileges, avenge* thy- Mat. 5. 38.
self, *an eye for an eye, and a* Lev. 19. 18.
tooth for a tooth, and love only thy neighbour : *Grace* lives by this *law,* Deny *thyself,* forsake *lands, life, houses,* take *up the Cross,* if he take thy *cloak let him have* Mat. 5. 40,
thy coat *also,* love *thy enemies,* 44.
bless *them that curse thee ;* when *thou art reviled revile not again,* 1 Cor. 4.12.
when *thou sufferest threaten not.* 1 Pet.2.23.

4.

The Gospel Method of Victory.

SUFFERINGS are ways of *victory* in another *method* and *form;* he that conquers under persecution, receives in the *enmity, wrath,* and *opposition* of his enemies into *himself,* and there *quenches* it and *destroys* it in Spirit ; for the *Christian* being one with the *Lord Jesus, flesh of his flesh, and bone of his* bone, is par- Eph.
taker of that *power* and *glory* which was in *Christ;* ·and *through him*

(who hath overcome the *world*) we
Rom. 8.   are *more than* conquerors, and this
1 John 5.4.   *is our victory, even our faith ;* and
the *strength* and *life* of *C*hrist is
shed abroad through all his *People*,
so as *death* hath no sting for them,
and the *grave* no victory over them,
1 Cor. 15.   the *violence of fire is quenched,*
Heb. 11.   *mouths of lions stopped, kingdoms
subdued.*

5.

How Resistings in some are of Flesh, and of the Law of Nature in others.

RESISTINGS are ever from
want of *conformity* to the
will of *God ;* and though *God* order and dispose all the ways of *man*,
Rom. 8. 28.   and act them to his own *purpose*
and *glory*, yet the *weakness* and
selfish courses of man are no way
excusable because of that, for man
acts from a *principle* of his *own*,
and of *flesh* contrary to that *revealed* and *manifested* providence
that God held forth to him, and in
that he *originally* and *naturally*

departs from *God*, and becomes a *god* unto himself, judging *good* and *evil* for himself, which is the *tasting* of the *forbidden tree*, and *seeks out many inventions.*

Thus it is in some, yet in others it is from that very *law* of *nature* and *self-preservation* under which they live and are acted.

6.

The Advantage Christians have of Bondage.

THERE are times of *bondage* which *God* hath for *his*, and through which they must pass into more spiritual liberty and enjoyments of Jesus Christ; for God hath this design, to increase his Acts 8. 1, *Gospel* by scattering such as pro- 2. fess it amongst other people, that the *earth* may be *filled with knowledge*, and to make his own *fulness* the portion of his *people*, and to carry them through some conformity to the *flesh of Jesus Christ*, even the *fellowship of his sufferings and death*, which is most *spi-*

F 2

ritual, as it is most in*ward*, and in *Spirit* or *sinful flesh*, but as it is more outward and carnal, as in persecution; so it is a *figure* or *image* of the more *spiritual*: and further, the *bondage* of God's people, according to this account I speak on, is in the type of the *Jew's* bondage, when the *Chaldeans* were to take *Jerusalem*, *Jeremiah* told them, *he that goeth forth to the* Jer. 33. 2. *Chaldeans shall live*, and shall *have his life for a prey;* and *go forth,* says he, *to the King of Babylon's Princes and live;* but if ye stay in the *City*, ye shall be consumed, which is a *figure* or *shadow* of abiding longer in any *dispensation*, or *way*, than God is clearly in it, and his *presence* appears upon it.

7.

Upon what Account the purest and freest outward Liberty is.

THE *People* of God shall receive their best and purest *outward liberty* upon another account than their own *strength*, *de-sign*, and *activity*, and that is by these ways.

The *glory* of *Christ* and the *light* of God shining more in their *faces* and *outward man*, the *nations* shall bring their *glory* unto them, and shall take hold of the *Skirt* of *him* Zech. 8. 23. *that* is a *Jew*, and say, we *hear that* God is in *you*.

The *meekness, peace, love,* and *righteousness* that shall appear from them, as *beams* from the *Sun*, shall much prevail upon the world, which are those only *graces* that the world can *love* and be enamoured on in God's people, for they are *graces* that go out to the *blessing*, and *prosperity*, and *preservation* of the *world*, and in such a *dispensation* as this, it is, that all men *love God*, because he appears to them in *things* of their own *nature*, his *Sun shining* upon the unjust, and his Mat. 5. 45. *rain* upon the *wicked*, and in such a dispensation it is that men shall *love* the people of *God*, while they shine upon them in such things as they can *bear* and *love;* though still according to another *Revela-tion* of *them*, or *manifestation* of

God in *them*, they shall be hated, as they do *God* himself.

And the other way for liberty is the *power* of *God* upon the hearts of *Princes* and *nations*, of which *Cyrus* and *Darius* were figures: Jer. 52. and the King of Babylon lifting *up the head of Jehoiakin.*

And that other way is the *Spirituality* of God's people, raising them from the love of worldly Interests and Engagements, save only for *righteousness* sake, and the *good* of *nations* in *administration* of *judgment* and *peace*, and when *Christians* appear to the *world* more disengaged from the *love* of *power*, *Dominion*, *Riches*, earthly *glory*, and the nations find them not in their own *ways*, nor desiring to live with them in their *borders* and *fruitful plains*, nor seeking their *vineyards*, nor plucking *apples* from their *trees;* their *jealousy*, revenge, *enmity*, in part and *persecution* shall cease towards them; the other way is, *God* shall make *Jerusalem* a *burthensome stone*, and a *cup of trembling to all nations*, they shall be weary of afflicting them, because of the *affliction* that shall come upon them where they are carried away *captive;* and the *Philistines* were a *type* of this, when they found the *Ark* of *God* plaguing them with *Emrods*, and they were to send it away with an *offering.*

8.

A Word concerning Heresy and Schism.

SOME *books* have been writ against me and I have been silent, and was rather willing to sit under the shadow of another's *contradiction* and *reproach*, than to reply, till *God* by his *Spirit*, in the hearts of such as did oppose, might bring forth *my righteousness as the noon day;* and then we, who had been enemies through the several measures of *light* we see by, and judging each other rather in *flesh* than *Spirit*, might rejoice and embrace as *brethren* in the *unity* of the same *faith;* and I saw further, that in books of controversy I left my adversary still upon some account with me for *passion* and recrimination, as all others do on all sides, whom I see write; therefore I rather made it my choice to Isa. 26. 20. enter *into the chamber* (or retirement of Spirit) *and shut the door upon me till the indignation be over-past;* for we can set but *letter* to *letter,* and *Scripture* to *Scripture,* and *argument* to *argument,* and *interpretation* to *interpretation,* and nothing can be judged till the *day* or *time* of more *revelation* of *truth,* till the *Holy Ghost* and *fire* sit upon *each of us,* trying every man's *work* of what sort it is, and *burning* up that in us which is *hay and stubble;* for writing *book* after *book* in such a *line of Replies* and *Rejoinders,* hath usually more of *man* than *God* in it, and *we seem to say with our lips we will prevail, our tongues are our own, who is Lord over us?* I am not against *contending for truth* earnestly, but that is in *Spirit,* not in *flesh,* nor *passions;* and I know well that the *Spirit* of *God* is flowing in, and is a *fire* in the *bosom,* but still as a *refiner's fire* trying and *purifying,* not *scorching* nor *burning* up that which is *pure* and *spiritual* in one *another;* and I know some allowance there must be on all sides to *infirmities* and *darkness,* and several conceptions of *truth* in all, which yet hath not been; and I know not any of us that either *preach* or write on *Scriptures* in such a *light* of *Spirit* as the *Apostles* writ the *Scriptures.*

Heresy.

HERESY is a *choice,* in the ἀίρεσις. signification of the *word,* and in the *application* of it in *Scripture,* it is a *choice* of some other *thing* for *truth* than is *truth,* by those who seemingly received *truth,* though after they make another choice of that which is contrary to *truth.*

    Heresy, which was judged by the *Apostles* accordingly, was a *choice* of some thing contrary to the *faith* and *sound doctrine* of *Scriptures* delivered by inspiration, or in *Spirit* and *Truth;* so as *Heresy* is something against the very *Doctrine* of *Faith* in the *Word* or Maik 7. 9. *Scriptures,* not against any *inter-*

pretations, doctrines, conclusions, glosses, Comments, or *Preachings* of men, who speak not *Scripture,* nor the *word of truth* originally nor *infallibly,* as the Apostles did; but so far as that is the very *Scripture* they speak, and so far as they speak the *truth* in *Jesus;* and in the *Spirit* of *God,* else they *teach* for *Doctrines* the *Traditions* of *men.*

Schism.

SCHISM is a breaking off, a renting or dividing from *Christians* who are in an outward profession of truth, and in an outward *fellowship* of *truth.*

Now there may be *Schism* in visible *C*hurches or fellowships of Saints upon this account, but there can be none in the true *body* of *Christ,* or the *spiritual Church,* which is baptized *by one spirit into one body,* for they *that are joined to the Lord are one Spirit,* and they are *made perfect in one;* and so far as they are in that *one Spirit* cannot be *divided,* nor can suffer any *Schism;* so as the dividing from *men* merely, or the *fellow-ships* of men merely, or the errors of *men*, or departing into higher *attainments* of *truth;* while the rest of the visible fellowships sit still, is no *Schism*, for if so, the *Protestants* were a *Schism* to *Rome*, and *Presbyterians* to *Bishops*, and all that go on from *faith* to *faith*, from *glory* to *glory*, to the rest whom they leave behind.

9.

Truth.

THERE is but one *Truth*, and that is *Jesus Christ; I am the way, and the truth*, and he is *Truth* in the *original* or *pattern;* and we see nor know no more *Truth* than we *see* and *know* in him, this is called the *truth as it is in Jesus:* For Jesus *Christ* is the *Alpha* and *Omega* of all things, and comprehends all *essence*, and *form*, and *life*, and *Spirit* of things in himself; and all things of this *Creation* are but Shadows and Images of this *Truth*, and the outward *forms* of that *glory;* this *Truth* makes *free*, John 14. 6.

that is the *operation* of it; and
therefore so much of *Truth* or of
Christ any one knows or receives,
so much *freedom* or *liberty* they
receive, and so much they are *delivered into the glorious liberty of
the Sons of God;* and where the
Spirit of *the Lord is, there is liberty :* And therefore as *Truth* is
in any, so is *spiritual liberty*, and
the Spirit of *bondage* in them passes
away, and such are disburdened of
the legal *terrors, fears*, of the *lies,
delusions, false* conceptions, *traditions* under which they have lived
as they grow up into *Truth;* the
Spirit of *Truth* only *teaches* and
reveals this *Truth;* and opens those
treasures of *wisdom* and *knowledge*
which are in *Christ. Truth*, though
it be but one, yet it shines forth in
many *streams* of *glory*, and opens
like *day;* in Jesus Christ this variety
of *truth* appears that *truth*, or *glory*,
or true *brightness* of God, and all
that *truth* of this *Creation* or *forms*
of the world; and all *truth* of *Letter*,
or *Scripture*, or *outward Ordinance*
is in its pure *Essence* and *Spirit* in
Jesus Christ; *Truth* gathers up
men more into *Christ* from the *flesh*

and loose vanity of the world; and
therefore we are said to have our
loins girt with *truth;* the *girdle* of Eph. 6. 14.
truth, as it were, binding us up,
and keeping close in Spirit to the
Lord; there is a *fulness, settlement,* and *establishment* in *truth,*
as in things of this world; there is
a far more *solid* and *real* enjoyment
in the *substance* of *things* here than
in their *shadows, counterfeits,* or
pictures, because there is a *nature,*
or *Spirit* and *life* in that thing to
be enjoyed, and answers the Spirit
and life of him that enjoys, by communicating something substantial,
solid, and *proportionable* than
images and *shadows* are. So it is
in the *truth, Jesus Christ,* in whom
is *life,* and more *excellent, glorious,*
and *spiritual* form, or *life,* exceeding the *nature* of things here, and
communicating more *true* and *solid
glory,* than all things here, which
are but as shadows to that, as other
things are shadows to them; therefore, says *David, I shall behold
thy face in righteousness; I shall
be satisfied when I awake with thy
likeness,* as if the *face* or likeness
of God, which is *Jesus Christ* the

image of the invisible God, could
only satisfy ; and the soul in such
a prospect of *light* and *glory* is truly
awakened, till when, it is but asleep
and in *dreams* and *visions* of its own
spirit, all the life and discoveries of
sense and *reason* being but *dreams*
rather than *true* awakenings ; and
therefore the more any one hath
seen of *truth* in *Jesus*, the more
spiritually and *highly* they judge
of all outward things, being not
satisfied in the mere *letter* or *form*
of them, but in the *spirituality* of
them, and true life of them, which
is *Jesus Christ.*

The *Mystery of true Christian Liberty from God, not from Man, or the Power of Men.*

WE have hitherto filled much
paper with *Scriptures, Reasons,* and *Arguments* for *Liberty*
of conscience, and thus far it hath
been well in order to the *peace* of
those whose consciences in *outward
things* run cross, *contrary,* and
destructive to others, both in *rule*

and *practice*, so as when *Christians* are under several *forms* and *administrations*, and these diametrical, or opposite to each other, and mutually *contradicting* and *expelling* each other, here can be no Peace nor Preservation of all, but from an *indulgency* or *liberty* in all; and this is such a liberty as *men* may give to *men;* this is the liberty of the *outward man*, and is upon the old *legal*, and *first Gospel* or *New Testament* account, as in the mere *letter*, as in those Scriptures; but this is yet below the true *Christian Liberty*, and a mystery unwritten, which is *originally* from the Spirit of *God*, and is merely *spiritual*, and works from a pure enlargement of *Spirit*, and a true *spiritual* Prospect of all *outward things*, which is an *image* of that *liberty* which is in God, who appears under his several *forms* of Creation *pure* and *holy* in *himself* or his own *nature*. But this is a *mystery* yet, and a *land* of peace and *purity*, not yet clearly discovered; nor the *right inhabitants* of it, but to some; and this *liberty* will further appear as the *Lord Jesus* is more and more revealed in the *Saints, judging* the world in *Spirit*, and reigning over the *tyranny* and *power* of men in a *glory* of *Spirit*, which shall *judge* and *torment* their *adversaries*, while they shall triumph over all the *practices* in the *flesh* against them.

A Discovery of the highest Attainment of the Protestants generally in the Mystery of Salvation.

Gen. 1. *A*DAM was the first *man*, created after *God's own* i*mage*,

Gen. 2.
1 Cor. 15. 48. he was a *public person*, and •he *sinning*, *sin* entered upon *all*, and

Rom. 5. 12. *death* by *sin;* the *Law* was after-

Exod. 20. wards revealed by *God* to 'Moses, wherein was a *copy* of that first i*mage* or *righteousness* from whence

Rom. 5. 12. *man* fell, and under the *condemnation* of which all *mankind* were by *nature*, or as born of their first *Parents*.

The way of life or salvation, which was revealed to be a way

Rom. 5. 19. out of this *condemnation* and *death*,

was by *Jesus Christ*, the *Son* of *God*, born of a Virgin in the *fulness* of time made under the *Law*, Rom. 8. 3. Luke 24. 46, 26. and fulfilling the *Law*, bearing *our* sins, crucified, *dead*, *buried*, and risen, *ascended*, and *entered* into Heb. 9. 26, 24. glory, and sitting at the *right hand* of God, making intercession for us; and by the *Preaching* of this *Jesus Christ* in the Ministery Eph. 4. 8, 9, 10, 11. of the Word which he hath set in his *Church*, a true and lively *faith* is begotten in the hearts of men, such as are *elect* or *chosen* in Rom. 10. 17. Eph. 1. 4. *Christ* before the *foundation* of the world was laid, not from any *works* foreseen, but of God's mere grace; and by this *faith* so begot- Eph. 2. 8. 9. ten, they apply *Jesus Christ* and all his *merits* to *righteousness* and Rom. 3. 22, 28, 25. *justification;* and through this, and the sanctified use of all other ordinances of God, as *Preaching*, 1 Cor. 1. 18. *Prayer*, *Sacraments*, the regenerate are more and more sanctified, and so built up in *graces of faith*, 2 Pet. 1. 5, 6, 7. *repentance*, *love*, *new obedience*, and made to persevere through the power of God unto salvation: *Nor* is the *Ministery* of the *Law* use- Gal. 3. 24. less in this, the Law being a part

of this *Ministery* to bring men to
*C*hrist, or to make them seek out
for *mercy*, they discerning their
misery by the preaching of the
Law, it being God's usual method
in Scriptures not to offer the *Gos-*

Mat. 11.
28.
pel without this *preparatory* of
humiliation and contrition; and
men so *humbled* and wounded by
the *Law* are only fit for the *mercy*
of the *Gospel* or of *Jesus Christ*..

Act. 1. 11.
This *Jesus Christ* they believe
to be one ascended according to
that *body* he appeared in, and
sitting at the right *hand of God*,
and in the figure of *glorified flesh*,
according to which all the *Saints*

1 Cor. 15.
shall be glorified in their *souls* and
bodies; and in Jesus *C*hrist thus
glorified in *flesh*, and entered thus
into his *Father's glory*, they believe; and to the Lord Jesus in
this *figure* and *form* of glory without them they are carried out in
faith; and through Jesus Christ
thus they believe that they are *justified*, and through the *Spirit* of
God in this *Jesus Christ* they are
sanctified.

Of Faith.

FAITH, they say, is a *grace* wrought by the *Spirit* of *God*, whereby a *believer* rests upon Jesus Christ for *justification*, and this they call *faith* of *adherence;* and when this *faith* works through love, obedience, *self-denial*, and other *fruits*, they call it faith of *assurance;* for, they say, *assurance* is obtained through the *Spirit of God* bearing witness in promises and *good works*, as well as by itself; and faith, working thus, is *sanctification* too, or *holiness* wrought by *graces.*

A further Discovery as to Free-Grace.

THEY believe *Jesus Christ* ascended in the *body* accordingly, and glorified in *flesh;* and through *Jesus Christ* thus ascended, and sitting on the right hand of *God* in this *figure* and *bodily form*, they accordingly conceive all *graces* of *Spirit* to flow forth

G

into the *Saints* in *faith, love, obedience, &c.*

But they look not on *justification*
as flowing from *Christ* acted upon
by the *faith* of a believer first, and
so a consequent of *believing* or of
faith, but an *antecedent* or going
before *faith;* they hold Jesus *Christ*
to be *righteousness* and *justification* to a *sinner*, and that all are
justified before they believe or *repent;* faith and repentance are
fruits of *righteousness* or *justification, Christ* being given to open the
Luke 4. 10. *eyes of the blind, and to bring the
prisoners out of prison, &c.* and
that all such *righteousness* and
justification clothes the *sinner* so
completely through *God's imputation*, that all *sin* is done away like
Ezek. a *thick cloud*, and none imputed to
believers; Christ hath taken away
1 Pet. 2. 24. all *sin* by his *offering* up *one sacri-
Heb. 9. 24, *fice* once for all; and that *faith* in
26. the *believer* doth nothing, no not
instrumentally as to *justification*,
but as by way of *revelation* and
manifestation of that *justification:*
Hence it is that they affirm no *believer* ought to pray for *pardon of*

sin, being a *righteous person,* at once in *Christ,* and *wholly pardoned;* but all this *righteousness* and *justification* they take upon the account merely of *God's imputation,* of *Christ* without us, or in heaven, who calleth *things that are not* as if *they were;* and they look upon all *works* and *duties, &c.* as *works* flowing from *love,* and from *justification* or *righteousness,* not directed to *justification* or in any order to it; we *believe, repent, love, and obey* (say they) not that we may be *saved,* but because we are *saved;* and any other *way of believing, obeying, &c.* they look upon as *legal,* and not so purely *Evangelical;* and they hold forth all the work of *justification* and *righteousness* to be of mere grace, and that all Gospel promises are *free;* and *Christ* is freely offered to *sinners* as *sinners,* in the *Ministery* of the *Word.*

So as their highest attainment is this, that God doth all to *sinners* in mere *grace;* that no *sin* is imputed to *sinners,* but they are pure only by imputation; and so no

Ezek. 16. 6, 7, 8. Eph. 2. 6. 8, 9. 1 Cor. 1. 30.

1 Pet. 2.
24.
Isa. 53 6.
Luke 1.
74, 75.

2 Cor. 5.
14

Matt. 9.
13.
1 Tim. 1.
15.
believers are punished for *sin*, but from *sin :* and all works of grace in a believer is because they are saved, or pardoned, not that they may be saved or pardoned; and all they are to do is from *love*, not from *bondage*, or from a mere *outward Commandment;* and the *Gospel* or *grace* of *God* in *Christ* is *free*, and in *free promises ;* and so to be *preached* to *sinners*, as *sinners.*

See Confession of faith made in this Assembly.

Confession of the seven Churches.

Articles of the Church of England.
They, commonly called Presbyterians, Independents, Anabaptists, &c. hold all points of doctrine, as to *justification, sanctification, faith, &c.* the *ministery* of the *word* and *Sacraments*, which they call *means* of *salvation ;* all these hold alike with the *common Protestant;* this being the sum of the *Articles* of the Church of *England* made by the *Bishops* and confirmed by Queen *Elizabeth*, King *James*, and King *Charles :* and there hath been no *Reformation* further, nor any higher attainment in these things, than the Bishops made, and the *Synod* in *England* formerly.

And all the *Reformation* that hath been endeavoured, hath been only in some outward things, as *Discipline* or *Church-government,* and some outward ordinances of *Baptism,* and the *Supper,* not any purer or more glorious discoveries of *God,* or the *Spirit,* or *Jesus Christ,* or our union with the *Spirit,* or *glory,* as to *spiritual* things, or *Christ* risen, but as to *Christ* in the *flesh,* or under the *law,* of which these or*dinances* were a *sign.*

A Discovery as to the general Point, or Christ dying for all.

THEY say the Scriptures hold forth all *sinning,* and *Christ* dy*ing* for all, and the *promises of Christ* generally to *all,* upon con*dition,* and *exhortations* to all to repent, *believe* and come to *Christ;* and therefore conclude the Lord *Jesus* or *second man* was given from the *Father* to give a price of Rom. 5. 12. 19. 2 Cor. 5. 15. John 3. 16. 2 Pet. 3. 9.

redemption for all those who fell
in the *first man;* and those, they
say, were all *mankind,* and with
Christ a *Ministery* of reconcilia-
tion and *graces* to all that will not
wilfully *reject,* or refuse, or put
by the *offers* of *grace* and *salva-*
tion so tendered, but remain *pas-*
sive, and so far as in them *lies,* not
oppose the *Spirit* and *means* of
grace, though they acknowledge
they can do nothing of themselves
to obtain *faith* or any other *work*
of *salvation,* but all that is merely
of the *Spirit of God* working in
those who are *called;*- and upon
these general terms of *grace* they
affirm also the *election* of some
which they conclude from that
work of *God* in them who are
called of God through the *means*
of grace, they not *resisting* that
call, or present *offer* of *grace.*

And this they say is the *Gospel*
of *salvation* preached to *all,* which
all may receive if they resist not.

Mat. 23.

2 Pet. 3. 9.

John 1. 11.

2 Pet. 3. 9.

The last Discovery, and as some say, the highest and most glorious, concerning the whole Mystery of God to Men, and this Creation.

GOD being infinitely *one*, yet in a three-fold manifestation to us, of *Father, Son, and Spirit,* would make out himself in an *image* in this *Creation*, or *nature*, and therefore he takes to himself *one part* of it into *union* to *himself*, according to one *way* of *manifestation*, called in Scripture *light*, *love, grace, salvation, father, bridegroom, glory*, and that part of *nature* which enjoys *God* in this manifestation of *grace* or *salvation*, is called the *Angels*, the *Saints*, the *Elect*, the *Son*, the *Tabernacle* of *God;* the *new Jerusalem*, the *Temple*, the *Spouse*.

Psal. 36 9.
1 John 2.8.
1 John 4.8.
Tit. 2. 11.
1 John 3.1.
John 3. 29.
1 Pet. 1.12.
Heb. 1. 7.
Eph. 1.1.4.
1 Cor. 12.
12.
Rev. 21.2, 3.

He takes to himself the other part of the *Creation*, and there he is *present*, but not in this way of *grace* and *light*, but of another *manifestation* called *law, justice, wrath, everlasting burnings;* and these are called *devils, wicked men, flesh,* which live in *God,* and subsist in *him* as *creatures* in their *being,* but not in his *grace* and *glory,* not in that *manifestation* of his, the *light shining in darkness, but the darkness comprehending it not.*

Psa. 139.8.
Acts 17.28.
Col. 1. 17.

John 1. 5.

This is the *mystery God* is in, as to this *Creation* and the brighter part of it, as to *Angels, Saints;* and to the darker part of it, as to *devils* and *wicked men;* and *all* that *God* doth here below, under the *Sun,* is to *preach* this in several *ways* or *ministrations,* as in the *appearances* of this *Creation,* in *light,* and *darkness,* and in the *Scriptures.*

John 5. 39.

The Scriptures are no other than a way or ministration by *letter* of this mystery, and all the passages there, from the first *man* to the *second,* from the *Old Testament* to the *New,* with those two very appearances of the *two men* or *Adams,* were but a *ministery* or *way* of *God* to signify or *figure* this *mystery;* and so all the rest

Gen. 1.
1 Cor. 15.
47, 48.

we read of, as of *Cain* and *Abel*, Gen. 4.
Isaac and *Ishmael*, *Jacob* and *Esau*, Gen.
Israel and *Judah*, *Saul* and *David*, 1 Sam.
Judas and the *Eleven*, *Christ* and Acts 1. 25.
Antichrist; and thus these set forth
and *figure* this *mystery*.

They say *Adam* was a way by
which God preached first to *man*,
and was not the first *man* in whom
all stood and fell, but a way by which
this *mystery* of *God* was made to
appear first to the *Creation*, and
Adam held forth *nature* or a part
of this *Creation* in communion with
God as to *grace* and *love*, while he
stood, and another part of the *Creation* or *nature* out of *communion*
with *God*, as to *love* and *grace*,
but in communion or union to God,
as to *law* and *justice*, or *wrath;*
and thus they interpret those *Scriptures* of *man's* first *glory* and *fall*
less in the *very letter*, and more
in the *mystery*, and according to
Adam, in this two-fold *state*, were
all the rest, *Cain* and *Abel*, *&c.*

They say that *God* in the *Old
Testament* preached this mystery,
though more darkly, and in *sha-
dows*, as in the *law*, and *sacrifices*, Gal. 4. 21,
and in the children of the *bond-* 23, 24, &c.

woman, and of the *free*, of *Israel's* walking with *God*, and *apostating*.

And that the *Gospel* or *fulness* of *time* of the *clearer* discovery of this *mystery* was the *Lord Jesus himself*, or *God manifest* in the *flesh*, or as in *one man*, a *figure* of the *whole mystery* as to *grace* and *love*, or *God in flesh*, or in his; or of *God* in that other *part* of his *Creation*, his *Church* or *Saints*: And all that *God* did in this *single* and *particular* manifestation in *flesh*, as in one *man*, was only a more full, clearer, excellent, and spiritual Ministery of the mystery of salvation; therefore *Christ* is called a *Minister*, one *sent*, an *Apostle*. And all that *Christ* did Luke 4. 18. from his *childhood* to his *crucify-* Heb. 3. 1. *ing*, *death*, and cross, was a discovery of *God* by this *figure* in the whole *mystery*, how *God* is in all *his*, and how he *works*, and hath his times of *law*, of *graces*, and Gospel, of crucifying and offering up all to *death* through the *eternal Spirit*, which is the *blood* of Heb. 9. 14. the everlasting *Covenant*, or *Seal*, whereby *God witnesses* to his people that he is their *God*, and they

his people, by killing all the *strength*
and *life,* and *power* of the first *Creation,* and carrying it up into a more
excellent and glorious *life,* his own
Spirit.

And so all Christ's *birth, growing,*
submitting to or*dinances,* cruci-
*fying, death, burial, resurrection,
ascension,* were so many discoveries
as to us in the *flesh,* of the *whole*
mystery of *God* in the *Saints,* made
out in these parts and *degrees,* and
several *ages* and con*ditions,* to shew
how God weakens and brings to
nothing the *life* of *nature,* or of
this *Creation* in which he will dwell
and make his *Tabernacle,* and carry
it up into a higher and more excellent *life,* even himself and his John 17.
own *glory.* 22, 23.

So, as they say, all that is spoken
of *Christ,* as in that *person* that
was *born* of a *Virgin,* who was *circumcised, baptized, crucified, dead,*
and *buried, risen,* and *ascended,* is
spoken in *figure* of the whole *nature*
into which God *enters,* or is born
into the *world,* and so takes our
nature along with him through
several *administrations* into *glory.*

So as the sum of all is this, that

the Lord takes our nature or this whole *Creation* into *union* with himself, and is *present* with it, in two ways of manifestation, of *grace* and *salvation*, of *Law* and *Justice;* and thus God is present with the *Angels* and *Saints;* with *Devils* and *wicked men;* and *Adam* and *Christ* are the two *eminent* and *principal administrations* of this *mystery*, and all the rest from *Cain* and *Abel*, through all the other several *persons*, or*dinances*, and *ministeries*, as of *Prophets, Apostles*, Antichrist, are but divers administrations or discoveries of this ; and all or*dinances, gifts*, and *graces* of the *Spirit* are but weaker appearances of this *mystery*, and such ministrations as the *Spirit* of *God* administers in our *nature*, till it be *glorified* in a *higher glory :* when

1 Cor. 13. 8—13. that which is *perfect is* come, that which is in part *shall be done away;* God shall be unto us broad rivers and *streams*, where shall *go no ship with sails*, nor *galley with* oars.

An additional concerning Antichrist and the Mystery of Iniquity.

THESE Scriptures hold forth a description of Antichrist.

There shall arise false Christs and false Prophets, and shall shew great signs and wonders. Mark 13. 22.

—Except there come a falling away first, and that man of sin be revealed, the son of perdition, who opposeth and exalteth himself above all that is called God, or that is worshipped ; So that he as God sitteth in the Temple of God, shewing himself that he is God. 2 Thes. 2. 3, 4, 9.

—Whose coming is after the working of Satan, with all power and signs, and lying wonders, and with all deceivableness of unrighteousness.

And as ye have heard that Antichrist shall come, even now there are many Antichrists. 1 John 2. 18.

And I beheld another beast coming up out of the earth, &c.—— Rev. 13. 11, &c.

And he doth great wonders, so

that he maketh fire come down from heaven——

And deceiveth them that dwell on the earth, by the means of those miracles which he had power to do.

And he causeth all, both small and great, &c. to receive a mark in their right hand, or in their foreheads.

The great whore that sitteth upon many waters.

Rev. 17. 2, 3 &c.   *I saw a woman sit upon a scarlet-coloured beast, full of names of Blasphemy, having seven heads and ten horns, and the woman was arrayed in purple and scarlet colour, and decked with gold and precious stones and pearls, having a golden cup in her hand full of abominations, and upon her head written, mystery Babylon the great. And I saw the woman drunken with the blood of the Saints.*

John 4. 3.   *And every spirit that confesseth not Jesus Christ coming in flesh —is that spirit of Antichrist.*

From all the *Scriptures* and the revelation of the *Spirit of God* concerning the *mystery of ini-quity* these things will arise.

That the mystery of iniquity or Antichrist is a false *Christ,* or false *anointed one,* that is, when any other thing but the *Lord* himself is in the *place* or *office* of *Christ* ἀντὶ pro vice *or* adversus. unto us, either our own *righteous-ness,* as our *Priest and Sacrifice,* or our own *wisdom, wit,* or *reason,* as our *Prophet,* and *Teacher,* and *Interpreter* of *spiritual things.*

And this *mystery* of *iniquity,* or *Antichrist,* is from a *falling away* first, that is, from a depar-ture from God, and the life and light of God, and *dependency* or *subsistence* in *God,* that is, when *man,* or the *spirit* of *man* will sub-sist of itself, live in itself, and be *wise* of itself, and *worship* of itself, and be *righteous* of itself; this is the *man* of *sin,* or *son* of *perdition,* or *flesh* which *God* will *destroy;* and this *Spirit* of *Antichrist,* or *man fallen* thus from *God,* sits in the *Temple* of *God* as *God;* that is, is in all *forms* of *worship,* and there *lives,* and *reigns,* and rules the whole *man* into a fleshly *obe-*

dience; and his coming or appearances are as *Satan,* that is, in *spiritual* wickedness, *transforming* himself into an *Angel* of *light, teaching, interpreting, revealing* the *mysteries* of *God* in carnal *reason* and *wisdom* by natural *parts* and *arts,* not in the pure *Spirit* and *anointing* of *God,* and so performing all things, in order to *God* and his *worship,* and *communion* with him, by lying signs and *wonders,* and *all deceivableness* of unrighteousness; for while the *spirit* of man, in its own *wisdom* and *power,* acts in the *pretence* of *God* and to *God,* and in the mighty *working* and *power* of *Satan,* it doth bring forth *signs* and *wonders,* even things *wonderful* in the *eyes* of the *natural* man; and such things as are very *signs,* very *images,* and *shadows* of *Spiritual* things, though not the things themselves.

And the *appearances* of this *man* of *sin* are many and divers, therefore called many *Antichrists;* and as this *man of sin* opposes the *Lord Jesus* in *spirit* and *light* he is called the *beast,* that *ascends* out of the *earth*, or the lowest part of the *Creation*, the *flesh;* and by the *fire* or *fleshly* counterfeitings of the *Spirit*, which he works in the sight of them that dwell on the *earth* or of those that are in the *flesh*, he *deceives;* And yet such is the *power* of this *beast* or this *spirit* of *flesh*, as it constrains *men*, and *compels* them, and overcomes them wholly to its own *power*, making such in whom it reigns to receive a *mark* in their *hand* and *foreheads*, that is, to *own* and *profess* this fleshly *wisdom* and *actings*, and to practise and put forth the power of it against *Christ* in *Spirit*.

And this is that *whore* too, for when the *spirit* of *man* is departed from *God*, and the *life* of *God*, it is become an adulteress, having left its *first love*, or *husband*, which was the *Lord* himself, and sits upon a *beast*, even upon the *flesh*, a *beast* of *scarlet colour*, that is, *bloody* and *persecuting* the precious and spiritual appearances of the *Lord Jesus*, and this is a beast of *seven heads* and *ten horns*, which *heads* and *horns*

are but figures of carnal *wisdom*
and *power*, and the *seven* and
ten figures of *perfection* and *com-
pleteness*, as to the *man of sin;*
for the *number* of the *beast* is the
number of a *man*, and yet his number is but 666, that is, is but a
number of weakness and *imperfection*, and *work*, or *bondage;* not
the number of *God* or of *seven*,
which is *perfection* and re*st*.

And the *whore* is adorned with
gold and *pearl*, which are those
excellencies of *nature* and *forms*
of *worship* and *Scriptures* with
which she *decks* herself, and is
adorned as a counterfeit *spouse* of
Christ, and upon her *head* is *mystery*, that is, all this appearance of
hers, even her *highest* and *choicest*,
her *head*, is *mystery* to all, who
are made drunken with the *cup* of
her *fornications*, or spiritual *whore-
doms* and *idolatries*, they discerning none of these, but all being in
mystery to them.

And this *Antichrist* is one who
denies *Christ* coming in *flesh*, or
God in his *people*, who is *coming*
and *coming*, that is ever flowing
out in *fresh* and *glorious discove-*

ries and *manifestations* of himself, forbidding all beyond them as *new lights* and false *revelations*, and fixing *God* and his appearances in their *Conceptions*, *Votes*, and *Results*, and *Counsels*, and Consequences, and *Conclusions*, and *Laws* of worship.

This Antichrist thus described is found in *man*, or the *spirit* of *mere man*, in all his *departure* or *falling away* from *God*, in all his lying *signs* or *counterfeitings* of the *spirit*, in his sitting as *God*, in his being a *beast* or opposing the *Spirit*, in his *scarlet* colour, or his crucifyings of *Christ* in us; in his denying the *Lord's* coming or further *manifestations* of his *light* and *Spirit* in us, and thus *quenching the Spirit.*

And from hence he flows out and spreads himself in the world in all Idolatrous *forms* of *worship*, in all false *interpretations* of *God*, and of the *truth* as it is in *Jesus*.

These are the several Attainments.

The Common Protestant.

THE common *Protestant*, as to
doctrine and *fundamentals*,
are so far in a discovery of the
mystery of *salvation*, as to behold
a *state* of *condemnation* in *sin*, and
a *way* of salvation by *Jesus Christ*,
and *faith* in him; yet some take
this way to be but a knowledge of
Christ after the flesh, and of *Christ*
as one single *person* or figure of a
man, and the first *glimpse* of the
love of *God*, and but merely a *discovery* beyond the *law;* and all
but a *fleshly spirituality.*

The general Redemptionist.

THEY that are for *general redemption* through *Christ*, in
the free offers of *grace* to all, and
his *dying* for all, some say, attain
no higher in this than *Christ* after
the *flesh*, and fall into the same
consequence with those that hold
the particular *election* and repro-

bation of some; and though there be in this a more general ministration of *Christ* held forth according to the *letter*, yet they say it goes not so high as the *mystery* of *Christ* in *Spirit* and in pure *glory* and *truth*, but of *Christ* in *glorified flesh*, and as in one single *person* or *figure* of a *man*; and all end but in a *fleshly* spirituality, and in an attainment as to the mere *letter* of Scripture.

The Free-Gracian.

THEY that have discovered up into *free-grace* or the *mystery of salvation*, singled out from *conditions, qualifications, and works,* some say, attain no higher in that than a discovery merely beyond the common *Protestant*, both going no higher than a *justification* by imputation, and through *Christ* after the *flesh*, as in one *single person* or figure of a *man* glorified in *flesh*, or the *body* without, and in a *local* glory, or a circumscribed nature, and putting all the *righteousness* upon a mere account in God, and all the taking away of sin or sinful *flesh* upon a *non-imputation* or *not-accounting* not in the cruci-fying, death, or *fiery trial* of the *flesh*, and the pure, *spiritual*, in-corruptible *seed* of *God* within, *Christ in us the hope of glory.*

And their highest attainment, as to *duties* and *works*, is only, as some say, to the *nature* and *manner* of their *production* or *flowing* forth, they counting the *nature* and ori-*ginal* of all no *higher* than a habit of *grace* or *quality*, and their pro-ceeding as immediately in the na-ture of that which they say is *love*; all they do being from *love*, and in *love*, not in *bondage.*

Conclusion.

AND these *attainments* are not such as are therefore con-demned, because no *higher*, or more *spiritual*, but are only considered as not the *highest*, but in order to the mystery of salvation, and several measures and ages of attainment, and seeing darkly, as in a glass, till that which is perfect is come.

A Discovery of Prayer.

THAT which hath been discovered concerning *Prayer* is this : First,

That they who could not pray in the *Spirit* might use a *form* of *prayer*, as *John taught his Disciples*, and the *Lord Jesus* his, in that of *Our Father, &c.* and *David* in the *Psalms;* and the *Apostles* and *Christ* himself are found in the same *form* and *expressions* of prayer very often : *he went away and prayed the same things again; Moses* prayed, *arise, Lord, &c.* and again, *arise, Lord;* this is the *first discovery,* and is *truth,* though *truth* in *weakness* and *infancy.*

A further discovery is, that prayer is rather a work of the *Spirit* than of any *form,* and that no set *form* ought to be put upon the *Spirit* of God, but what it freely *breathes* and *speaks,* and all constant *speakings* to *God* in this (as they call) a conceived way, or *impremeditate,* or *extemporary* way is taken commonly amongst *Christians* for *prayer* in the *Spirit,* and for that *spiritual* way of *prayer* which the *Disciples* of *Christ* used in the Gospel, who were grown up from the *infancy* and *childishness* of *forms* or *words* taught them, which is but a mere *natural* or *outward* thing, as they say, which any may perform by strength of natural parts, as *wit*, and *memory*, and *affections*.

The furthest discovery as some say, is this :

That *Prayer* is no other but the *revelation* of the *will* of God, or *mind* of God, as to *such* and *such* particulars, either *spiritual* or *temporal*, and is an immediate, *proper*, and *spiritual* act of the *Spirit* of *God* in the *Saints*, and that all such *speakings* as are not from the very *manifestation* of the *Spirit of God* in us, are but such *prayers* and *petitions* as natural *reason*, and *memory*, and *affections* may *form* and *dictate*, and doth usually ; and that there is no difference betwixt such kind of *praying* and *forms* of *prayer*, (though it may be *extemporary* or *conceived*, as some who can pray upon this *account* three or four hours, and nothing more *frequent* now ;) nay, this kind of

Rom 8. 26, 27.

prayer is far worse, by how much it *transforms* itself more into an *Angel* of *light* and is not, sitting in the *Temple* of *God* as *God;* or pretending itself to be the *Spirit of God,* and is not, being more properly the *flowings* and *breathings* of *reason,* and the strength of *man's* wit, and *memory* and *affections,* and is constantly performed in *public* and *private,* and thus *fire* is fetched down from *heaven* in the *sight* of *men* that dwell upon the *earth,* or such as are yet more *below* than above, or in *heaven,* and *Spirit:* and thus the people of *Israel* Isa. 1. prayed, whose *prayers* were an *abomination;* thus the *Pharisees made* Mat. *long prayers, &c.*

So as *Prayer* then, according to this *discovery,* is the *Spirit* of *God* only *revealing* and *speaking* in the *people* of *God,* we know not what *to pray for* as we *ought,* that is, Rom. 8. *we,* as *we* are *ourselves* know not: 26, 27. And therefore all that we pray, and not the *Spirit* of *God* in us, not that Spirit of *Prayer,* spoken on in *Scripture,* is but the *Spirit* of man *praying,* which is but the *cry* of the

H

creature, or a natural *complaining*
for what we want, as the *Ninevites*,
and the children and *beasts* of that
City all cried unto the *Lord*.

But in pure *prayer* the *Spirit*
helpeth our infirmities, the *Spirit*
of *God* which makes *intercession*
with *groanings* which cannot be
uttered; that is, the *speakings* or
manifestations of the *Spirit* of *God*
are not so utterable by the *flesh* or
voice of *man*, and the *Spirit* maketh
intercession for the *Saints* according
to the *will* of God, or according to
God, (as in the Greek) that is *Prayer*
is *God* speaking in us his *mind* and
will; And therefore the *Lord Jesus*
taught this in that *form* and *doctrine* of *his:* Thy *will be done in
earth as it is in heaven*, wherein
he set forth that more *spiritual* and
perfect *Prayer* which was only according to *God*, and which the
Saints should *pray* afterwards when
the *Spirit* was more revealed.

And this is *prayer* in *Spirit*, and
to pray thus is to pray in some *evidence* and *demonstration* of God,
and in *faith* or *believing* the will of
God, as to *this* or *this* thing, at *this*

Rom. 8.
26, 27.

or *this time;* whatsoever *ye ask in prayer, believing, &c.*

And all other *askings* or *seekings* of God which are not thus in *Spirit,* and in the *will* or *mind* of God in some *evidence* or pure work of Spirit, or raising of *Spirit,* is but the *askings of creatures* as *creatures;* and thus all mere natural and carnal *people* pray, and are heard and answered many *times,* in the *mercy* and *goodness of God,* who makes *his Sun to shine upon the just and unjust.*

All *exhortations* in *Scripture* to this *duty* of *prayer,* as *seek ye my face, pray* continually, *watch* and *pray,* be fervent in prayer, *ask and ye shall have, &c.* are only then rightly, *effectually,* and properly *applied* and *obeyed,* when the *Spirit* of *God* doth it in the *Christian,* when the *Spirit* of God breathes in and reveals the *will* of *God,* and acts in the *duty* or expressions, and the *Christian* speaks in himself, or in presence of others, that *mind of God;* and so this Spirit of *God* clothes itself in flesh, or *letter,* or expressions, as to the *outward man;* and they who say *Amen* in the *Spirit,*

ás the *Apostle* saith, say *Amen* in
the same *Spirit,* or else they are
not in *prayer* in a pure *spiritual*
closure, or *unity of Spirit.*

Prayer is the *workings* and *weaker*
or fainter *manifestations* of the
Spirit of *God* in the *Christian,*
while he is in *bondage,* that is, while
God is not the *fulness,* the *light*
and *glory,* and *all* in *all* unto him ;
for where there is any *asking,* or
seeking, or desiring, there is not
*perfect rest, enjoyment, all-suffici-
ency,* and *fulness :* And therefore
while *Christians* are in *bondage,*
and not yet brought into the glorious
Rom. 8. *liberty* of the *sons of God,* they are
under the *Ministration* of *Prayer* to
God, or of *asking ;* as children are
to a *father* in nonage and pupilage.

All *Scriptures* of *Prayer,* or
John 16. concerning *Prayer,* and the *prayers*
23, 24. of the *Saints* in the vial, are con-
siderable respectively to the state
Rev. 8. 3, of weakness and bondage the Saints
4. are in, praying not in the *Spirit* of
God, but in *weakness* or the *flesh,*
according to their own *wills;* which
hath been usual with *Saints* formerly, as *Paul,* who prayed *thrice*
to remove the *buffeting,* and was

answered, my *grace* is sufficient *for thee*, or is it not enough that I have *grace* for thee in all my *dealings* and *dispensations* towards thee, live thou upon *that?* and the *Lord Jesus* himself prayed, Father, *if it be thy will let this cup pass;* yet afterwards he was more the *manifestation* of God, Father, not as *I will*, that is, not as *I*, or that of *man* in me, but as *thou* wilt; and many *Christians*, wanting the clear and glorious *revelation* of the *will* of *God*, pray for *such* and *such* things, for the *obtaining* such and such *mercies*, and *removal* of such and *such miseries*, being all this while in the *dark* to the *will* and *mind* of the *Lord;* when, as if the *will* of the *Lord* were seen or discovered, they would *rejoice*, and be at *rest* in such *conditions*, and learn how to *want* as well as to *abound*, that is, to *want* such or such things as the *Lord* takes from them, and to *abound* in the *Lord* without those things, or with *those things*, which is the sweet *state* of the *Christian*, and a *rest* or *peace* in figure to that *glory* and *fulness* to be *revealed* in us, and those *Christians* as are in

2 Cor. 12, 7, 8, 9.

Mat.

Phil. 4. 11, 12.

some measure in this *light* or *glimpse* of the *fulness* of *God,* are entered upon the *borders* of *Canaan,* and are feeding upon some *bunches* of the *grapes* of the *promised land.*

A Discovery of the Law.

SOME say, the *Law* is obligatory and binding to all *Christians,* because moral, and so perpetual, and that it was re*vealed*

Gal. 3. 19. because of *transgressions* : And that the *Law* is of no less *efficacy*

Rom. 7. 7. now than before to reveal *sin* and convince of sin, and that *Christ*

Mat. 5. 17. came not to *destroy* the *Law,* but to *fulfil* it; that the ministery of the *Law* ought to precede and go before the *Gospel,* because none ought to have *Christ* offered to them in a *promise,* but such as the *Law* hath *humbled* and *prepared;* that *God* doth *sanctify* the Ministery of the Law to *conversion* and *sanctification* of his *people,* and such as *preach* it are not *legal;* thus the *Protestant* in general.

Others say that a further *discovery* of the *Law* is this.

That the *Law* was a discovery or appearance of *God's righteousness* and *man's*, according to the *nature* of both, as in the first *Creation*, God is revealed in the *Law* to be *one God* and only to be *worshipped*, and no other *Gods* but *one;* and *man* is *revealed* in his first created *righteousness*, love thy *neighbour as thyself.* Mark 12. 32. Exo. 34. 14. Luke 10. 27.

The *Law* is in every one by *nature, accusing* and *excusing,* and God's transcribing it into *tables* of *stone,* was to set before man a testimony or *witness* in the *letter* of what *Law* he had inwardly, the *Law* is *spiritual,* and to bear witness to his *Apostacy* and *falling away,* and to all his *sins, transgressions* and *enormities* committed. Rom. 2. 1. Rom. 7. 14.

Moses and the *Prophets* were *Ministers* of it in the *letter,* the *Law* was given by *Moses,* it being first delivered or preached by the *Ministery* of *Angels,* or *dispensation* of *Angels;* the Lord Jesus himself and the Apostles were *clearer* and more *spiritual Ministers* of it. John 1. 17. Mat. 11. 13. Heb. 2. Math. 5. Rom. 3. 31.

The Law, as it is in *letter,* and in the *Ministery* of *Moses,* and Heb. 10. 1.

the *Prophets*, and *Christ, &c.* is a
witness and i*mage* to the more ex-
Rom. 8. 2. cellent *Law*, that of the *Spirit* of
life in Jesus *Christ*.

The Law, in mere *letter* and
Rom. 8. *legal ministery*, works *bondage*
15.
Heb. 2. 14, and brings forth the *spirit* of *bond-*
15. *age* in those who are under the
Law, working *convictions* and *tes-*
timonies of *good* and *evil*, whereby
the *law* of *nature* is awakened
Rom. 2. 15. and *strengthened* to accuse *sinful*
flesh.

The Law, as it is a *figure*, or
shadow, or i*mage* of *Spirit* or *spi-*
ritual righteousness, may be a
Ministery of *preparation* or *wit-*
Mat. 3 3. *ness*, as *John* was, *prepare ye the*
way; and the Baptism of *water* to
an outward *purification* or washing
as the *letter* or Ministery of the
Law is; and this is a *Ministery* of
God's first *appearance* to a *sin-*
ner.

Men may work very high, as to
God and *duties* and *works* by the
Ministery of the *law* or *letter*
without, and the *law* within, and
the *letter* of *Scriptures* interpreted
by no higher a *light* than that of
the *law;* and yet all such *right-*

eousness is but to *bondage*, compared with the higher *law* or *Spirit* Rom. 8. 2. of *life*.

The *Law* curseth all *unright-* Rom. 3. 19, *eousness* as to the *flesh* or *man* 20. *sinning*, and it is that *standing* condemnation of *flesh* or *sin;* the *Law* was revealed because of *trans-* *gression*, and *cursed is every one* Gal. 3. 10. *that continueth not in all things* *that are written in the Law.*

All the *repentance* and *reforma-* *tion*, which the *Law* or mere *mi-* *nistery* of the *letter* works, is not *spiritual* but *legal;* and yet, if in *order* to a more *spiritual* or to *Christ* in Spirit, it is of the *nature* of *John's* Ministery, a *preparatory* John 1. 17. and *figure* of more *glory* and *truth* Heb. 10. 1. in substance.

The *spiritual* man, who lives in the Spirit, is not under the mere *law* of the *letter*, but it is according to its *spirituality*, the *princi-* *ple* and *spiritual life* of him, so as such are not under the *Law* but Rom. 6. 14. under *Grace*, and not in *bondage* Rom. 7. and *fear* but *love; perfect love* 1—6. 1 John 4, casting out *fear*. 18.

They that are true *spiritual* comprehensive *Christians* know in what order and subserviency to place the *law*, as it is in a ministery of *letter*, when as the *Infant Christian*, in the first discovery of *Christ* or *Free Grace*, looks upon all *Ministrations* below him as *legal*, and so is carried out to oppose them too disorderly.

A Discovery of Duties and Works.

S OME say that duties and works are *fruits* of *faith* and
of the *habits* of *grace* in us, and

Gal. 5. 22.
Col. 1. 10.
Mat. 7. 16.
Mat 5. 16.
Mat. 28. 20.

are the conformity of a *Christian* to the *Commandments* and *Laws* of *God* revealed in *Scriptures*, and that *duties* are to be done because

1 Tim. 6. 18.
Heb. 10. 24.
James 2. 14, 18.

commanded, and that they are such *ways* and *means* as God hath appointed a *Christian* to walk in to *salvation;* and that according as these are performed more or less

1 Cor. 11. 28.
2 Cor. 13. 5.

strictly a *Christian* ought to *judge* himself or *approve* himself, and that *Christians* are to wait upon *God* in *duties* for the *Spirit* and for all other discoveries of himself thus the *Protestant* in general.

Others
works of a
Spirit of *C*
tion, else tl
ances and
not of so
of God.

That
or *letter*
to a *Chr*
in *duties*
our *heart*
this is the
performar
Testame
New, or
nant, the
a *Minist*
Christ fr
in the *let*
figures of
doth act fi
in him, n:
him, nor
hell; bec
actings
as first f
nary or
tion,

Others say that the *duties* and *works* of a Christian flow from the *Spirit* of *God*, of *love* and of adoption, else they are but the *performances* and *obedience* of *servants*, not of *sons* and such as are *born* of *God*.

Rom. 5. 5.
Luke 1. 74.
2 Cor. 5.
14.
Rom. 8.
15.

That the mere *Commandments* or *letter* of *Scripture* is not a *law* to a *Christian* why he should walk in *duties*, but the *law* written in our *hearts*, the *law* of *life;* and this is the *difference* of duties and performances under the mere *Old Testament dispensation* and the *New*, or pure *Gospel* or *new Covenant*, the one or that of *Moses* was a *Ministery* from *without*, that of *Christ* from *within*, and that *duties* in the *letter* are but *Images* and *figures* of what the spiritual man doth act from that *life* of *Christ* in him, not as things *commanded* him, nor in relation to *heaven* and *hell;* because such *obedience* and *actings* are of *service*, and acted as first from *without*, and *mercenary* or of *price*, and for *salvation.*

Rom. 6.
14.

Rom. 7.
1—6.

A Discovery of outward Ordinances.

SOME say, outward *Ordinances* are *Commands* of *Christ*, and therefore to be done because they are *Commands*, and that they are *sanctified* by *God*, and his *Spirit*, and that we are to wait on *God* in the use of *means*, and that spiritual things are conveyed by Ordinances into the *souls* of *men*, thus says the *Protestant* generally.

Others say, That outward Ordinances as in the *letter* are the *Old Testament* Ministration, or a *Legal* ministration of *John's* ministery, or *Christ* under the *Law*, or in *flesh*, and that such *Ordinances* as the Lord Jesus commanded while he was in the *Ministery* of the *Law* made under the *Law*, a *minister* of circumcision, and not commands of *Christ* as in mere *glory* and *spirit*, nor a ministration of his as in that more excellent *condition* and the not distinguishing *Christ* as in *flesh*, and so *teaching* and com-*manding*, and as in *Spirit*, and so

ministering in *pure spiritual light*
and *glory*, is the reason of all such
legal doctrine and *use* of ordi-
nances in bondage, as is this day
in the *letter*: Other of Baptism,
&c. or *Church fellowship, &c.*

That the *new Covenant* or *God*
revealed in his, and teaching *his*
is not by any *outward* way or *ministery* or *means*, but by the *inward* or *unction* and *anointing*, ye Heb. 8.
are all *taught of God;* no man
shall *teach* his *neighbour* or *brother* any more, saying, *know* the
Lord; and all con*ference* and discoveries in *letter* or *speech* is but
mere witnessing to the *Lord* and
the *discoveries* of *God* of what we
are *taught*, not any *ministery* (as
formerly) for *teaching.*

*N*o outward *ordinance* or *ministration* of the creature or of *letter*
can con*vey* or confer or bring in
pure *spiritual things*, there is a John 3. 8.
great mistake in that, and they are
but *signs* and *shadows* of *spiritual* 2 Cor. 4.
things, and they are to the *Spirit* Heb. 10. 1.
in the *New Testament* as the *sha-
dows* of the *Old* were to the *flesh*
of *Christ*, figures and *perishing*

Col. 2. 20.
1 Cor. 11.
26. things and to be fulfilled in *Spirit* and in the coming of *Spirit*.

They are that which are called

1 Cor. 13.
12. the beholding *God* as in a *glass,* the *seeing darkly* and *in part* the *heavens* and *earth* which are to be rolled up as a *garment.*

A Discovery of the Jews and their Conversion.

SOME say, they are those who are of the seed of *Abraham* and have *Abraham* to their *Father,* and are *Jews* by *fleshly* birth, and such as live yet in the Old *Testa-*

Rom. 11. *ment* Laws and *Privileges* as cir- *cumcision,* and have the *veil* upon

Rom. 9. 6, their *hearts* untaken away, oppo-
7. sing *Christ* come in the *flesh,* and expecting the *Messiah* yet in a more carnal *glory,* they shall be *converted* and *called* in before the coming of *Christ* in *Judgment.*

Others say, That the *Jews* were but a *figure* of the *children* of the *bondwoman,* and of the *Christians* under the *Apostacy* or in mere *let- ter* and *corrupted forms* of *wor-*

ship; and as the *Jew* was reckoned before to be the people of mere *Ordinances,* and of the worship of *God* according to the letter of *Scriptures,* to whom the *Oracles of God* were committed, and to Rom. 9. 4. whom pertained, &c. so the Christians generally who are now the people of the *New Testament,* as to *letter,* and of all the worship according to the *scriptures* in the *letter,* are that *Jew* under the *new Testament,* answering to the *Jew* under the *old,* there being two *seeds* according to the flesh and Rom. 9. 6. according to *promise,* though they 7. by *promise* or *faith* are counted for the *seed.*

The calling of the *Jews* is the Rom. 2. bringing up the *Christians* from 28, 29. *letter* to *Spirit,* and according to this mystery the *Jews* shall be *called* and *converted* daily; and are; for in the whole *Nations* of *Christians* as of *Italy, Germany, Poland, Denmark, Spain, France, Scotland, England, &c.* the *Lord* shall call in many by his own Spirit into himself, and shall be revealed in them in *power* not in *form.*

That the *Jews* who are by *nature* Jews or according to *fleshly generation* shall be no otherwise called but as the other *Jew* of which they are a *figure;* and thus they interpret the *call* of the *Jews* and not in any such *outward* observation as *men* commonly suppose, not remembering that the *kingdom of God* comes not with *observation* as to the world, and that the day of the *Lord* shall come as a *snare* upon all the *earth.*

Rom. 11. 28.

Luke 17. 20.

All *false* Worships and Ways, *practised* in Conscience or in Liberty, will be destroyed in Christ's Day.

GOD hath a time before *Christ* come in *Spirit,* as he had before *Christ* came in the *flesh,* a *time* wherein he *suffered* long and was *patient,* and was revealed to his people, though dwelling in much *Gentilism, Judaism,* and *ignorance;* and therefore *God's appearance,* or *communion* with his *people,* from the time of the *falling* away, or of

the man of *sin* being revealed, hath 2 Pet. 3. 3,
been in *grace* and *long suffering,* 4, 8, 9.
and hath patiently borne his being
cruc*i*fied in spiritual *Sodom* or
Egypt, and therefore he hath been
with his people under *Popery,* under
Episcopacy, and is at this day, not
in approbation of their *form* but in
his own mere *love, grace,* and *long-
suffering,* and is at this day accordingly with the *people* in *Independency, Presbytery, Baptism,
&c.* and all other *male-administra-
tions.*

 The Lord Jesus hath a *day* and 2 Thes. 1.
time to be revealed in, which is his
coming in the *Saints,* when he will
judge the *World,* and then shall
Antichrist be consumed, and the 2 Thes. 2.
flesh of the *whore,* or *Babylon* in
all her *administrations* shall be tor- Rev. 17.
mented and burnt with *fire,* and not
a little one of *Babylon* shall be
spared, but dashed against the *stones,*
not the purest *Idols* she hath, even
Idols of *gold* and *silver,* with all
her merchandize, *pearls,* and *precious stones,* and *cinnamons* and
odours, and *frankincense,* all things
of *false worship, &c.* and *administration,* though very *sweet* and pre-

cious in the *judgment* of *flesh* and
blood, and then shall all the *saints'*
Indulgencies cease to all these
things under which they are now
walking, some in *Conscience*, some
in *Liberty*, even then when God's
i*ndulgency* *ceases*.

A Discovery of Christ
in us.

SOME say it is no other but
habits of *grace* in us, and such
a *work* of *sanctification* and *mor-*
tification wrought by the *graces* of
the Spirit; and this they say is
Christ formed in us, the *image* of
Christ, the *conformity* to *Christ ;*
this the Protestant generally.

Others say *Christ* in us is when
we are made the *anointed of God*,
which is the *Christ*, or the *whole*
1 Cor. 12. *entire Christ*, as one *spiritual new*
12. *man.*

And that the *image* of *Christ* in
us is *Christ* manifested in our *flesh*
Phil. 3. 10. as to *sufferings* and *death*, whereby
the *flesh* is *crucified* in the *power*
of *God* and of the Spirit, and the
outward man or the *Flesh* is *dying*

and *perishing* even *day* by *day,*
and is then *dead* when the very *life*
of the *Flesh* is *slain,* and we *live*
no more unto ourselves, but *God* or
Christ liveth in us, it being no more
we that *live,* and *manifested,* as in Gal. 2. 20.
resurrection, or in the life of the
Spirit, wherein we who were *dead*
in sins and *trespasses* are risen with
Christ, who is the *resurrection* and
the *life,* I am *the resurrection and*
the life.

The Fiery Trial.

THERE is a State and condition
of Christians scarce known,
and it is the *fiery Trial,* or that
power of God put forth upon the
administrations that *Christians* are 1 Pet. 4.12.
under, and so passing out of them
into higher *discoveries* of *God;* and
the *fiery trial* is the Spirit of God
burning up or destroying such an
administration to a *Christian,* as
when a *Christian* passes from a
mere *legal state* into a state *less*
legal or more *Gospel,* receiving
some more precious and sweet *ap-*
pearances of *God* in *Grace,* and
free promises; in this passage there

is a *Fiery Trial* upon that first
Administration that was *Legal,*
whereby man's own righteousness
is consumed and *crucified* to a more
excellent discovery of *God;* and
even in that more *Gospel-State* of
a *Christian,* whereby he enjoys *God*
in that *ministration of graces,* gifts,
and *Ordinances,* there will be a
fiery Trial in a *Christian's* passage
into more glorious *manifestations*
of *God,* and there will be a *burning*
and *torment* even in that *ministration* of his *graces* and *gifts, &c.*

And this State is *Prophesied* of
in that Scripture, the sun shall be
turned into *darkness,* and the *moon*
into *blood* before that *great and
notable day,* that is, not only the
Lord Jesus, the *Sun,* (as some say)
will be as *darkness* to the *world,*
&c. but all that which was the *glory*
and *light* of a *Christian,* and his
way of communion with God, his
Sun, and *Moon,* and *Stars* shall be
darkened and become as *blood* before that *notable day,* or that more
excellent *revelation of God:* and
2 Pet. 3. 10. that of *Peter, but the day of the
Lord will come, &c.* in the which
the heavens shall pass away with a

great *noise, and the elements* shall melt with *fervent heat ; the earth also, and the works that are therein shall be burnt up ;* which is not only a *Prophecy* of the last *judgment,* but of the *particular judgment* upon *former administrations* in a *Christian* which is *figured* out in the *heavens* and *earth,* and *elements,* which are those *more* or *less glorious administrations,* and the *fire* is that *trial* by the *Spirit* of God which as *fire* burns and *destroys.*

This is accordingly *figured* out in that to the *Corinthians,* The fire *shall try every man's work, of what sort it is ;* If any man's *work shall be burnt, he shall suffer loss,* which work is those several *administrations* of *gold, silver, precious stones, wood, hay, stubble,* which pass under the *revelation* of the *day,* or *glory* of *Christ,* or *fire* of the *spirit.* 1 Cor. 3. 13, 15.

This is further *revealed* in *Revelations,* 2. 9. I know thy *works* and *tribulation* and *poverty, &c.* and ye shall have *tribulation* for *ten days,* this was written to the *Church* of *Smyrna,* or to all *Chris-*

tians under the *figure* of that *Church* which was *tribulation, prison* or *bondage* and *poverty ;* that is, while *Christians* are in their former *administrations* as in *bondage, prison, poverty,* looking at all they have as *nothing,* and all *former things* they were rich in as *nothing,* and now as *bondage* to a more excellent enjoyment of God.

This is likewise in the mystery of it, the cross *of Christ,* or the Phil. 3. 10. *fellowship* of Christ's *sufferings, crucifyings,* and *death,* for as *Christ* crucified all that glorious *administration* in which he was in the *flesh,* and it all *died* to a more *glorious life,* even the glory of *God* the *Father,* so every *Christian* is to take up this *cross,* and 1 Cor. 1. 17, to bring his *highest* and *choicest* 18, 23. *administration* to this *cross,* and 1 Cor. 2. 2. to have them all *crucified* to higher discoveries of *God,* this is the Gal. 6. 14. knowledge of *Christ Crucified,* or *self-denial.*

Many *Christians* who are *saddened, darkened,* in much *tribulation* as to the *administrations* they are under, and take them for *de-*

sertions and *withdrawings* of God, when as they are the *presence of God* upon such *administrations* making them dark and *wither* and *consume*, and the bringing in of a richer and fuller *glory*.

God in Heaven or in a Place of Distance as to our Infirmity.

MANY *Christians* in their conceptions of *God* and *prayings* or *addresses* to *God* consider him as in a *local glory*, and so *change* the *glory of the* incorruptible *God into an image made like to corruptible man.*

God is *infinite* and *all* in *all*, and whither shall *I go* (saith the Psalmist) from thy *spirit*, or whither shall *I fly* from thy *presence*, and where is the *place of his rest?* Isa. 66. 1. And say not in thy heart who shall *ascend into heaven to bring Christ* Rom. 10. *down from above?* The *word is nigh even in thy heart,* the *word* (saith the Apostle) that *we preach*, which *word* was *Christ* the eternal *Word*, which was with *God* and

was *God:* And thus the *Lord* is
Phil. 4. said to be *at hand,* the *Lord is at hand.*

The spiritual *Christian* knows that all *figures* of *place,* as of God's residence, as *heaven,* and all such discoveries of *God* as to *place* or *distance* are only as to *man* and to the *infirmities* of *man;* and therefore *prays* not and *speaks* not to *God* nor of *God* as to *Place* or *distance,* but as if he were in *him* and about *him,* his *right hand embracing him* and *his left hand under him;* and in such discovery of God as he hath by *faith, &c.* or any such *graces* and other *ad-. ministrations* he *worships* not *God,* nor considers *God* as *that* or *that discovery,* because then he should worship something for *God,* which is not *God,* and as *John,* fall down at the *feet* of the *Angel* or some glorious ministration and *worship* there.

The *carnal* and *weak* Christian *worships, prays, &c.* and thinks of *God* as to *form, figure,* and *place,* and *distance,* and *discoveries* of him by *graces, gifts, &c.*

Whereas *God* is only to be enjoyed in *those* as in a *glass* darkly, for *we have not seen his shape, nor heard his* voice.

The Spiritual Sabbath.

THIS *Mystery* of *God* was held forth first in the Creation in that of the *seventh day* which God was said to *sanctify*, Gen. 1. which was no other than the enjoyment of *God* in the *Revelation* of *himself*, who is perfect *rest* and *sabbath* in his own *glory*, the *six days* being accordingly a *figure* of the *Christian* in bondage or under *active* and *working administrations*, as those of the *Law* and *Gospel* are, as all forms of *worship, duties, graces, prayer*, Ordinances, &c.

This *Sabbath* was *a* sign to the people of God in *bondage* or under the *law*, and the *Lord Jesus*, in his *Active* and *fulfilling* Administration while he was in the *flesh*, was the *Antitype* of the *six days*, and his entering into *glory* was Luke 24. that very *Sabbath* and *rest*, which 26. was the *bosom* of the *Father* from whence he came and where he John 1. 18.

re*turned*, and this is the *scope* of
that fourth *chap.* to the *Hebrews*,
and the *bosom* of the *Father* is
that *Sabbath* or *Rest*, *there re-*
Heb. 4. *maineth therefore a rest to the*
people of God, and he *that hath*
entered into his rest hath ceased
from his works as God did from
his, that is, the *Lord Jesus* having fulfilled his day's *work* as to
the *law*, entered into his *glory* or
re*st*, so *Christ* in that held forth
the true Christian *Sabbath*, which
was the *father*, as *Philip, shew*
us the Father and it sufficeth us ;
there is *fulness*, rest, sabbath, and
sufficiency in the *Father*, or *Re-*
velation of *God* in the *Christian*.

So as the *Spiritual* Christian
in the true *discovery* of *God*, his
fulness lives in an *eternal* every-
day *sabbath*, while some live in
little more than the bare *sign,* or
one *day* in the *week*.

The Gospel as in its own Glory, and as in the Scriptures of the Old and New Testament.

THE *Gospel* is ever*lasting*, Rev. 14. 6. for it is the *tidings* and *Revelation* of *God*, in *love*, *grace*, or *mercy* to his, or *God manifested* in *flesh*, or making his *Tabernacle* with men.

This Gospel, which is no other than the *mystery* of *Salvation*, *revealed* or *declared* in Spirit to men, is clothed in several *administrations*, as that of the *Old Testament* and the *New*, the *Scriptures* of *both* being the *Revelation* of *heavenly* things by *earthly* or created things, or by *natural forms* and *expressions*, so as the *letter* is a *parable, figure* or *allegory*, by which *spiritual things* are spoken and brought forth amongst men; they are they which *testify* of *Christ, hitherto I have spoken to you in* Proverbs, &c. The *Scriptures* or *writings* of the *everlasting Gospel*, are the true *scriptures*,

as they are the very Image and
letter of the mystery of *Salvation,*
or of *Spiritual* things, or the *mind*
of *God*, or as they are in that pure
and *spiritual Order* and *form* of
words to truth itself; not as they
are merely in their *grammatical*
construction and sense or common
reading, which any that *understand* the *Hebrew* or *Greek* may
receive, and therefore the *Scriptures* according to *such* or *such
interpretations* and *consequences*
of men, are not to be imposed as
mere things of *faith* and *fundamentals*, but so far as the *spirit*
of *God* reveals them to be that
very *truth* and *mind* of *God* in
those who receive them, else they
are received and *acknowledged* for
the *Authority*, and reputation of
men, not of *God*, therefore *C*hrist
told the Pharisees they erred, not
knowing the *Scriptures*, and yet
they *had* the Scriptures, and *read*
them, and understood them in the
letter, but not in the *Spirit*.

The Gospel being ,thus distinguished into the *spiritual nature*
of it, and into the *administration*
with which it is *clothed*, nothing

is *pure, spiritual, divine Gospel,*
but that which is *light, life, glory,*
spirit, or *God revealed;* whatsoever is of mere *letter, form, Ordi-*
nance, is of the *administration* or
Gospel-clothing and *appearance,*
as to *men* and as in the *flesh,*
things that are seen are *temporal,*
things *that* are not seen are eternal.

So as that distinction used concerning *Ordinances,* when they are
called *Gospel-Ordinances, Gospel-*
Commandments in *contradistinc-*
tion to the legal *Ordinances* is a
great mistake and an *advancing*
and *Exalting* outward things into
spiritual, and putting an *Image* of
Christ and *divinity* upon them,
which they will not bear in such
an *opposition* or *contradistinction,*
to the *Ordinances* under the *law,*
for all the *Ordinances* under the
law or of the *Old Testament,*
were *Gospel Ordinances,* or *Ordi-*
nances holding forth *Christ,* and
figuring *Christ :* and so the *Ordi-*
nances of the *New Testament;*
and are all alike *letter, outward,*
and *visible,* and of things that
perish with using, which was the

Col. 2. 2. *nature* of the *Administrations* of
the *Law*, and therefore saith the
Apostle they did all eat the same
spiritual meat, and they *did all
drink* the same *spiritual drink*,
1 Cor. 10. and they *drank* of that *rock* that
3, 4.   *followed them*, and that rock was
Christ; that is, the *Ordinances*
of the *Law* or *Old Testament*
were as much *spiritual* as those of
the *New Testament*, that is, such
things as signified *Christ* in the
flesh, which those of the *New
Testament* as *Baptism*, and the
last *Supper*, but he concludes, be
not ye *Idolaters as were some of
them, they sat down to eat and
drink and* rose *up to play;* that
is, they did *Idolize* those outward
administrations as their *manna,
water*, out of the rock, and *pass-
over* which they *ate* and *drank*,
and ro*se* up to *play*, that is, lived
in the mere refreshments of such
formal participations and *communion* with mere outward things
and *Ordinances*, and were *cheered*
and *contented* with such *created
enjoyments* of God; thus they
rose up to *play* after their *Idolatry*
with those *Administrations*, as

many weak Christians now, who
having *sat down* to eat and drink
in the *Administrations* of the *New
Testament*, as these in the *Old*,
rise up to *play*, go away fed up with
created *refreshments*, rather than
spiritual *manifestations* of *God*.

Assurance *of* Salvation.

THE *pure, spiritual*, and *glorious* assurance of *salvation*
comes from the *knowledge of God*,
or the pure *manifestation* of the
Spirit of *God*, bearing *witness*, and
giving *testimony*, that we are the
children of God; this is *pure spiritual* assurance, this is called the
white stone with a new name writ- Rev. 2. 17.
*ten, which none know but those
that have it*, this is the *unction* 1 John 2.
whereby we know all things, this 20.
is that Spirit by which we know 1 Cor. 2. 12.
things freely given to us of God.

So as all Demonstrations of Salvation, which are made to the *soul*
by any *rational, persuasive*, or *Ar-
gumentative* way, and not in the
mere evidence of the pure *light* or
spirit of God, is but moral, or *human*
and *traditional*, and will fail; and

all applications of Gospel promises, and all *C*onclusions from the mere letter of Scriptures, which are not the pure image or Figure without, answering the very evidence and demonstration of *Spirit*, and of God within, is but a literal and *formal* assurance, and will fail.

All counterfeit or resembled testimonies, either by Satan, who can transform himself into an Angel of Light, or by the mere persuasion of Nature, or the carnal conscience, whereby *N*ature doth willingly deceive, and flatter and persuade itself, being usually unwilling to *perish*, and believe its own *destruction* will fail.

But there are many ways of *assurance* of *Salvation*, though more dim and faint, besides that more *inward* and purely spiritual, and that merely of God, which is enjoyed very *rarely*, and I know not by whom, excepting those only to whom the *Kingdom of God* is revealed in *spirit*, and *God* is seen *face* to *face;* and first *assurance* is wrought by the *knowledge of God*, according to such enjoyment as the soul is

under in its *Administration* to God,
as

First, there are these ways of *knowing* God.

1. By reason or the *mere* light of *nature*, and *works* of this *creation*, and here is a *law accusing* and *excusing*, (as the Apostle saith) and how God is revealed in this as to salvation in all those *Nations* where the Gospel is not heard as in its outward letter and Administration, or elsewhere, and how far God may administer *C*hrist in this, as formerly to *Job* and *Cornelius,* I dare not *judge,* nor *condemn,* nor *conclude,* but sure there is no *Salvation* out of *Christ;* and how far God may use this light of nature or reason to administer *C*hrist in, as he makes use of others more low and visible *administrations* not so excellent, I know not.

2. There is a knowledge of God by *graces* and *gifts,* or fruits of the Spirit, as faith, love, self-denial, repentance, &c. and by the letter or promises, and outward *Ordinances* and *Duties;* and as God's manifestation is in these, so is the assurance

of *salvation* through these, and such assurance is of no *higher* and *clearer* and more *glorious* certainty than God through these doth afford, that is, (as the Apostle saith) darkly as in a glass; and as these are sha-dowed and clouded, so is the assur-ance, and that is the reason why so many are cast down and afflicted as to this thing of *assurance,* and pine and consume because the *tes-timonies* of their Salvation are no brighter nor clearer than such Ad-ministration will admit, and here they are to wait.

The reason why *assurances* of *salvation* are no more *glorious* nor *pure,* is because the *spiritual Church* or Saints are in *Babylon,* in the *flesh,* compassed about with the *mystery* of *iniquity,* and of *Antichrist* in ourselves, and *enjoy* not *God* in that *sweet* and pure *vision* as they shall do when they return to *Jeru-salem,* the new *Jerusalem,* the *C*ity of the *living God.*

They that speak of the assurances in pure *revelation* of *Spirit,* not comprehending all the several *ad-ministrations* and *measures* wherein *God appears* to his, do much mis-

take, and it will appear from that
knowledge of *God* which is amongst
men, in all its several *dispensations,*
as here follows.

The Knowledge of God according to the various Dispensations of Himself.

GOD is known in the *light* of
nature or *reason,* and *works*
of this creation, the *eternal power* Rom. 1.
and *Godhead* being seen *by things
that do appear,* and *man* being
made after the *Image* of *God,* and
having a *law* within him *accusing* Rom. 2.
or *excusing.*

2. By the mere *letter* or *scriptures,* and *light* of *nature* or reason,
which is a *rational dispensation,
heightened* from such *Images* and
appearances of *God* as it meets with
there or in *letter.*

3. By *outward Ordinances,* or
signs and *Images,* and things that
do *appear,* and thus *God* is seen
still as in the *creation,* or *in created*
things.

4. By the *ministery* of *Angels,*
or a more *high* and *Seraphical,*

though still creature-ministrations of *God.*

5. By *graces* or *appearances* of the *Spirit,* as *faith,* repentance, *love,* self-denial, *humility,* &c. which was the *ministration* of the first *Gospel*-times under the *Old Testament,* before *Christ* came in the *flesh,* and now in the *New Testament,* since his *coming,* and this is said to be as in a *glass.*

2 Cor 3.18.

6. By *God's* own *light,* even *himself* revealed; and this is that *pure, increated, divine, immediate* glory, *flowing* from himself, or *himself;* FATHER, (saith *Christ*) glorify me with *thyself,* or the *glory that I had with thee;* and the *glory that thou gavest me, I have given them,* that they *may be one as we are one.*

John 17.

Now let us consider, who knows *God* according to *himself,* or his own *light* and *glory.*

None (saith God) *can see me and live;* so as they that see *God* do not live, they do not *live,* or that thing called *themselves* do not *live;* that which is called a *man's self* is his own *reason,* his *wisdom,* his *righteousness,* his *desires* or *will,* his *imaginations,* his *affections,* his *lusts;* now if these *live,* God was never yet seen, none can see *God* and *live;* for when any see *God,* it shall be no more they that *live,* but *Christ* or *God* that *liveth* in Gal. 2. 20. them ; now who is there that hath *seen* God that doth not *live,* in whom nothing of *self lives.* And that we may see how *God revealed* will *annihilate* and bring to nothing all *flesh,* consider the appearances of *Angels,* and *graces,* &c. How was *Daniel* smote into *astonishment?* no *spirit* was left in him : how was *Isaiah? Woe is me, I am undone, I have seen the Lord :* how was *John* when he fell at the Angel's feet? how have many left the world and worldly contents, relations, and all other creature comforts, as many *Anchorites* and *contemplative souls,* who are carried no *higher* than by *Angel* discoveries !

Oh! how doth the pure *appearance* of God pour shame upon all *flesh,* and *fleshly glory* and *excellency,* upon all the *visions* and *dreams* that man hath had of *God,* either by pure *reason,* his *image,* or by *creature-imagery,* or outward *administration* and notion by *letter,*

1 Cor. 13. or by *graces, &c.* for *when that which is perfect is come, that which is in part shall be done away:* The day of our Lord will be upon all our **Isa. 2.** *Cedars, and Oaks, and pleasant pictures,* and *Idols of gold* and *silver,* even our richest and most *spiritual Idolatry,* and *judgment* shall be upon all the *merchandize of Babylon,* the *pearls* and *precious stones,* the *Cinnamon* and *odours,* and *frankincense,* upon all *deceiveableness of unrighteousness,* and all false *worship, &c.*

A further Discovery of the Mystery of Salvation in the Gospel-Administration, and its own Glory.

THE *Gospel-administration,* wherein the *mystery of salvation* is first discovered, is in the Scriptures of the *New Testament* held forth in these following particulars.

1. In *repentance,* which they say is a *sorrow* for sin wrought by the *Spirit of God* and the *Law,* flowing from *Christ,* who gives *repentance*

to Israel, and the *Spirit of grace* Acts 5. 31.
which *mourns* over *him*, *&c.* and is Zec. 12.10.
that *godly* sorrow for sin, the *new-* 2 Cor.7.10,
man grieving over the *old.* 11.

2. In *faith*, which they say is
an *act* of the *regenerate soul* upon
Christ, resting and *believing* in him Rom. 3. 28.
for *justification* and *righteousness*,
or as some say, a *grace* from *Christ* Rom. 1.17.
or *righteousness.*

3. In *conversion* or *calling*, which
is the *work* of the *spirit* of God,
turning, or *sanctifying*, or *per-* 1 Thes. 4.7.
suading the soul of the *Christian* 2 Tim. 1.9.
from his *sinful* and *unregenerate* Psal. 19. 7.
estate to God in Christ.

4. In *justification*, which is God's
pardoning the *sins* of a *believer*, or Rom. 5. 9.
not *imputing* sins unto him, and Rom. 4.25.
imputing the righteousness of *Christ*
unto him, whereby he stands *justi-* Rom. 8.33.
fied and *forgiven*, and *righteous* in Rom. 5. 1.
the *sight* of *God freely ;* and of
God's *grace* through *faith instru-*
mentally, which as the *hand* receives *Christ*, as some say ; without
faith, as others say. Thus the
Scriptures in the *letter* hold forth
the first *revelation* of the *mystery*
of *God* in such words and expressions as these, and *such* as *these*

are, as *prayer*, good works, duties, ordinances, which are very *suitable*, and *proportionable* to the first *appearance* of *God* in *us*, or the *mystery* of *salvation*, working in its *infancy* and first *creation* in the *Christian*, and thus the *infirmity* of *Christians* is fitted with a *manifestation* of the *mystery* in *words* and *forms*, and all the *Christian* *Churches* of the world generally draw out all their *Systems* and *models* of *divinity* into *articles* of *faith*, and *Confessions* of *faith*, according to this very *letter* of *Scriptures*, which is no other but a *revelation* of the *mystery* of *Salvation* as to man's infirmity, and say some, they call it their *fundamentals*, and the highest *attainment* of *Christianity*.

Others say the *mystery of salvation* is no other than *Immanuel* or *God* with us, or God in *flesh*, not only in that man *Christ*, but in the whole *Christ*, *Christ* being no more but an *anointed one*, and that *anointed one* is our *nature* or weakness *anointed* with the *Spirit*, even God himself who is strength ; and this mystery of great and exceeding *glory* is revealed in *pieces* and *parts*, and after the *manner* of *men*, according to the *infirmity* of our *flesh*, within the *Christian* in *graces*, *&c.* and in the *Scriptures*, or *expressions* and *forms* without the *Christian*.

The Seekers, *their Attainment, with a Discovery of a more spiritual Way.*

THEY find that the former *Christians* of the *first* or of the *Apostles'* times, according to *Institutions* then, and the *administration* of *Ordinances* then, were more *visibly* and *spiritually* endowed with *power* from on *high*, or with *gifts* of the *Spirit*, and so were able to make *clear* and *evident demonstrations* of *God* amongst them; as in the *Churches* of all the *Christians* then, in *Corinth, Ephesus, &c.* And that all who administered in any outward *Office*, as to *spiritual* things, were 1 Cor. 12. *visibly gifted;* there was then an *Apostle, Evangelist, Prophet,* Eph. 4. *Pastor, Teacher, Gifts* of *Heal-*

1 Cor. 13. *ing,* *Gifts* of *Miracles,* of *Tongues,* *&c.* And all was *administered* in the *anointing* or *unction* of *Spirit,* *clearly,* *certainly,* *infallibly :* they ministered as the *Oracles of God.* But now in this time of the *Apostacy* of the *Churches,* they find no such *gifts,* and so dare not meddle with any *outward Administrations,* dare not *preach, baptize,* or *teach, &c.* or have any *Church-fellowship,* because they find no attainment yet in any *Churches* or *Church-ways,* or *administration* of *Ordinaces,* according to the first *pattern* in the *New Testament,* they find *nothing* but the outward *Ceremony* of all *Administrations ;* as of bare *water* in *Baptism,* of bare *Imposition of hands* in *Ordination,* of bare *Election* of *Officers,* as *Pastors, Teachers, &c.* of bare *Church-censures,* without the visible power of *gifts* of *Spirit* which were before.

Therefore they wait in this time of the *Apostacy* of the *Christian Churches,* as the *Jews* did in the time of their *Apostacy,* and as the *Apostles* and *Disciples* at *Jerusalem,* till they were endued with power from on *high,* finding no practice for *Worship*, but according to the first *pattern*.

They wait only in *Prayer* and *Conference*, pretending to no certain *determination* of *things*, nor any infallible *consequences* or *interpretations* of *Scriptures*.

They wait for a *restoration* of all things, and a setting up all Gospel *Officers*, *Churches*, *Ordinances*, according to the *pattern* in the *New Testament*.

They wait for an *Apostle* or *Angel*, that is, some with a *visible glory* and *power*, able in the *Spirit* to give visible *demonstration* of their sending, as to the world : and thus they interpret those places of the *Revelation*.

This is the *highest* of their *Attainment*.

But some speak of a further *discovery*, and more *spiritual* than this of the SEEKERS, as this :

1. That there is no warrant from *Scriptures* to expect any restoring of *Offices* or *Ordinances* according to the first *pattern* in *Scripture*.

2. That the first *pattern* in Scripture of *Offices* and *Ordinances*, was but a more *purely-legal Dis-*

pensation, or a discovery of the *Gospel* rather as to *Christ* after the *flesh*, than after the *Spirit;* and a discovery as to the weakness both of *Jews* and *Gentiles* then, respectively to *visible Administrations*, and gifts of *Spirit*.

3. That the *Administrations* and *gifts* then, were but a *ministration* in *part*, and *darkly, as in a glass*, and of things that should *vanish away*.

1 Cor. 13. 10—13.

4. That *God* never set up any *Administration* or *Office* but for a *time* and *season*, and used it as a *temporary dispensation;* as the *Tabernacle, Temple, Law, Priesthood, &c.* and then left them never to be *restored*. So the first *Gospel* administration by *Ordinances, gifts, &c.*

5. That to wait in any such way of *Seeking* or expectation, is *Antichristian*, because there is no *Scriptures* to warrant any such restoration, or *expectation* of such *administrations:* and that all such *waiting* is that *desert, wilderness-condition* prophesied on by *Christ;* that is, *waste* and *barren* as to *spiritual* things : *If they say, Be-*

hold, he is in the desert, go not Mat. 24.
forth: And that it is that condition
prophesied on to be in the *secret
chambers,* or *single fellowships*
that are in such expectations; a
chamber signifying an *upper* room,
or a room above others; so this *state*
of *Seeking* is thought by those of
that *Way,* to be an *upper room,* or
higher *administration,* as to *Presbytery, Independency, Baptism,
&c.* and that *Lo, Christ is here,*
or the gathering into that *Way,*
and saying it is *his,* to *wait in.*

6. That the *truth* is, *C*hrist is in
all *his* in *spirit* and *truth,* and as
the *eternal seed;* and his *fulness* Col. 1. 26.
is already in the *Saints,* or all true
Christians: and that all *growth,* Eph. 3. 18,
improvement, or reformation that ¹⁹·
is to be, is only the *revelation* or
appearance of this: *When he shall* Col. 3. 4.
appear, &c. or to be revealed in 1 John 3. 2.
the *brightness* of his *coming,* in the 2 Thes. 2.
day of the Lord Jesus; and that 8, 9.
he is *in us* that true *life, salvation,*
glory; only we see him but in *part;*
and that all conceptions of *God* or
Christ, as to distance of *coming,* Rom. 10. 6,
&c. administrations, ordinances, 7. &c.
gifts, are but to expect Christ in a

Col. 1. 26. *fleshly* way or appearance, not as he is *in us,* our *life, fulness, hope of glory, &c.* And this next *appearance* of his shall be in his own *light, spirit,* and *glory,* in *himself* and *his.* And this is that *Reformation* to be expected ; this is the Psa. 36. last *administration* of *himself* by *himself* in *his: In his light we shall see light.*

And the *Saints* or *true Christians* shall not only see *God* thus in *himself, face to face,* as they *are seen;* but the *world* shall see him in a way of conviction and *spiritual judgment* upon *themselves;* even *him that sits upon the throne.*

And all that pure *administration* of *Ordinances* and *Gifts* which was and is expected by these, is but a *middle* or *interdispensation* betwixt God and *his;* wherein God is seen as in a *glass,* not as he is in his own *glory,* which is *himself,* which is the last and most spiritual discovery.

The Grounds both against Liberty of Conscience *and for it, clearly stated, for all to judge.*

Against Liberty of Conscience *these are the strongest Grounds, and all the Grounds generally known.*

THE *Magistrate* is the *keeper* of *both* the Tables of the *Law*: and as he may punish any *evil* committed against the *second Table*, or the *society* of man; so he may punish any *Idolatry* committed against God, or the *Worship* of God, in the *first Table*. *Custos utriusque Tabulæ.* *Exod.* 20.

2. The Magistrates under the *Old Testament* reformed; *Moses* and *Joshua*, the Kings and Princes of *Judah* and *Israel*, *Nehemiah*, &c. so the Magistrates *now*.

3. The Magistrate is the *minister of God for good*, and *a terror to evil works*, and *bears not the sword in vain*; therefore may punish *Heresy* and *Schism*, because *evil*. *Rom.* 13.

4. The Magistrates are *prophesied* on to be *assistants* to the

Church of God : *Kings shall be thy fathers, and Queens thy nursing mothers;* and therefore may punish all such as are enemies to it, as all *Heretics* and *Schismatics* are.

Acts 5. 1.   5. *Peter* smote *Ananias* and his wife *Sapphira* with death, which was a *temporal* punishment for their *sin* of *Hypocrisy :* so may the Magistrate put forth a *temporal* punishment for a *spiritual* offence.

6. *Paul* wished that they *were*

Gal. 5. 12. *cut off which troubled them:* there-fore Magistrates may cut off *Here-tics,* because they are troublers of the Church.

Rev. 2. 18.   7. The Church of *Thyatira* was reproved for suffering *Jezebel* to teach, and to seduce : therefore Ma-gistrates are not to suffer *false Pro-phets* or *Seducers* to be.

Zech. 13.   8. The *father* and *mother* of him that is a *false Prophet, shall thrust him through, and say, Thou shalt not live; for thou speakest lies in the Name of the Lord.* This was a *Prophecy* as to Magistrates' punishment for *Heresy*.

9. If Magistrates shall not punish for *Heresy, Errors* and *Schism,* there will be nothing but Confusion,

and no settlement nor establishment of any *Peace*, *Order*, or
Truth in the Church.

10. It appears from the *practice*
of all *Christian States* generally,
who punish all such as conform not ;
from all *Councils* and *Synods*, who
still hold this power to be in the Magistrate, of *reforming* and *punishing Heresy* and *Schism*.

The Grounds for Liberty of Conscience *which are strongest, and
are all commonly known.*

1. *Moses* was a keeper of *both*
Tables only as he was a Type of
Christ, and so called the *Mediator
of the Old Testament*, and *Wor-* John 1. 17.
ship of God then : but so is not the
Magistrate now, the Office of
Moses being fulfilled in *Jesus* Acts 3. 22.
Christ, and ending in him, even
in that Person in whom all the Luke 9. 30,
Types were *fulfilled*.   35

2. The Magistrates of the *Old
Testament; as Moses, Joshua*, the
Kings of *Judah* and *Israel*, *Nehemiah*, *&c.* were in a peculiar and
special way of *Magistracy* as to
that *Church-Polity* of the *Jews*,
and had a *special*, and *peculiar*,

K

and *infallibly* directive power of *Priesthood* with *Urim* and *Thummim*, and *Prophets anointed* of God to *assist*, and *direct*, and *instruct* them in the *Law*, or *Reformation* of the Church at *such times* as they reformed. And the Law of

2 Cor. 3. 6, 7, 13.

the *Old Testament* lay more plainly and clearly in the *letter*, not so much in *spirit* as the *letter* of the *New Testament :* And therefore the Magistracy now having no such special reference to a *Church-Polity*, nor any such Ministery *infallibly* directive joined to them, cannot proceed so to re*form*, nor com*pel*, nor *punish*.

3. The Magistrates under the *New Testament* are Ministers as

Rom 13. 4

to *good* and ev*il*, not as to *Truth* and *Heresy :* and this *good* and *evil* is such *good* and *evil* as falls under the Law of *their* cognizance, that is, the Law of *Nature*, by which they *make* Laws, and *judge* the *breach* of them : which Law of *Nature* or *right Reason*, is the *Law* or *principle* for administration of *Justice* and *Righteousness* in all Societies of *Men* and *Nations :* And thus

Rom. 13. 4.

the Magistrate *bears not the sword*

in vain. But *this* is not as to *Heresy* and *Schism,* of which the *higher* Law is judge, *viz.* the *Law of the Spirit of life* which is in Jesus Christ, not the Law of *Nature* or this *Creation.*

4. In that Prophecy, *Kings shall be thy fathers, and Queens thy nursing mothers,* is not in its own Scripture, or any other, interpreted to be any other thing than the *indulgency* and *favour* of States and Kingdoms to the *people of God;* which is far from bearing witness to any *destructiveness* or *persecution* of them.

5. That *Peter* smote *Ananias* and Acts 5.1,2. his wife *Sapphira* with *death* for lying, is only a witness of God's power and holiness put forth in an act of *Miracle* upon the sin of Hypocrisy for *convincing* unbelievers, and *confirming* believers, and is no way *exemplary* to any Magistrate, being a power by *miracle,* or by an *extraordinary* act; and *Magistracy* in its *administration* is ordinary : and it was in an *Apostle,* not a *Magistrate,* by a *spiritual,* not a *carnal* weapon.

6. *Paul's* wishing that *such were* Gal. 5. 12.

cut off that troubled them, holds forth no other *cutting off* than by *Church*-censure or *Excommunication*, which was a visible *dividing* them from that visibly *spiritual body*, the *Church*, called a *delivering up to Satan, &c.*

Rev. 2. 18.   7. The *Church* of *Thyatira* was reproved for suffering *Jezebel* to *teach* and to *seduce :* but this is not the *Magistracy* of *Thyatira* which was to forbid her teaching by *punishment*, but the *Angel* or *Ministery* of that *Church*, as *all* agree, who was rebuked because they or he put not forth that spiritual power they had of *Admonition, Rejection, Excommunication.*

Zech. 13. 1, 2, 3.   8. The father and mother of him that begat the *false Prophet*, and was to thrust him through that *prophesied* lies in the name of the Lord, was a *Prophecy* respectively to the Law of the *Jews* which was amongst them against *false Prophets*, and had a *true* Priesthood, and *infallible* Prophets, with a *special* Law to *try* them by, and *condemn* them. And more *spiritually* was this : By the *false Prophet*, is meant the spirit of *Antichrist :* by the *father*

and *mother* that *begat* him, they
who *made* him a *Prophet*, or *begat*
and cried *him up* into the *reputation* of a *Prophet:* and then *thrust-
ing him through* for the *lies he* prophesied, is their spiritual smiting
that *Anti-christian working* with
the *Sword of the Spirit*, through
some new *enlightenings* from God
received, or *brightness* of Christ's
glory, which shall *slay* and *kill* all
appearances and *deceivableness* of
the man of sin or *false Prophet*,
and not suffer him to live.

9. That there will be no settlement of *Peace, Order*, or *Truth*
in the Church if the Magistrates
do not punish for *Heresy*, is upon
mistaken and false grounds, sup-
posing three things which are not.
First, that the *Church-polity* of
the *Jews* by *Magistrate* and *Priesthood* is to be used by *Christians;*
which is not, it being fulfilled in
Christ, the true King and Priest;
and *Christians* having no such *infallible* Priesthood to join to Magistracy. Secondly, that *Civil power*
can establish anything of an higher
glory, law and *principle*, than *itself*, as all spiritual *truths* and

discoveries of Jesus Christ are.
Thirdly, the mistake of true spiritual *settlement, peace, order,* and
truth, which receive all their *being,*
propagation, and *establishment*
from the Spirit of God, and the
Scriptures, and such spiritual Laws
as God hath revealed for ordering
the *outward man* of the *Christian*
by, respectively to the *Society* or
fellowship of other *Christians,*
called *Church-censures,* &c. *Chris-*
tians being under a twofold *Polity;*
that of the Kingdom of *Christ,* as
Christians; that of the kingdom
of this *world,* as *men,* or such as
are subject to the Laws of *civil*
Government: And likewise sup-
posing all *peace* and *order* to be
grounded upon *Uniformity,* not
Eph 4. 3. upon *Unity of spirit;* and preservation of the *civil* Peace of the
State.

10. That *States* and *Kingdoms*
do to this day *practise* punishing
Heresy by the power of *Magis-*
trates, and that Councils and Synods do allow it; all such *practice*
of what States soever in this kind
doth shew only what they do, not
what they *ought* to *do.* And the

kingdoms of the world are *prophe-* Rev. 17.17.
sied on to give their Kingdoms and
strength from *themselves* to the
false Church. And for *Councils*
and *Synods,* they are such as have
erred in o*ther* things, and why not
in *this?* It being their great *Interest*
to establish themselves, &c. by the
Magistrate's power.

Whatsoever is not of faith is Rom. 14. 23.
sin: So as all who are compelled in
things of *Worship* to do anything
of which they are not *persuaded,*
do sin.

Gospel-sins, or sins against an
higher law or *light* than that of
Nature and *Reason,* (which is the
only sphere for *Civil* Government
to move in) is to be *judged* and
punished by a *law* and *light* proportionable, and more *spiritual* than
any power of *Magistracy;* as the
Spirit of God going out in Gospel-
Judgment, *Admonition, Rejection,
Excommunication, &c.*

The danger and hazard of *Persecution* of the *members* of *C*hrist,
which is a sin bringing much *judgment,* because judged and punished
by such a *light* and *law, viz.* by
Synods and *Councils* of *men* who

are not infallible in their *decrees*
and *judgments* of *truth* and *heresy*.

By *force* and *compulsion*, men
who are *weak* in the *faith* are
made *hy*pocrites, in their *outward*
man conforming to the *laws* of men
in *fear* and *bondage*.

All such *power* of *compulsion* in
States and *Kingdoms* principled
with any *light* and *liberty*, except
Spain, *France*, *&c.*, shall destroy
the true Interests of all such *States*
and *Kingdoms* oppressing all *Societies* and *fellowships* of men, as
to *spiritual things*, though never
so peaceably affected, as *men* and
subjects.

A Mystery; or the Christian following the Appearances of God through all created Things.

T HAT which is the *pure*, *spiritual*, *comprehensive* principle of a *Christian*, is this :—
That all outward *administrations*, whether as to *Religion*, or
to *natural*, *civil*, and *moral* things,
are only the *visible appearances* of

God, as to the world, or in this creation; or the *clothing* of God, being such *forms* and *dispensations* as God puts on amongst *men* to appear to them in: this is the garment the Son of God was *clothed with* down to the feet, or Rev. 1. 13. to his lowest appearance. And God doth not *fix* himself upon any one *form* or outward *dispensation*, but at his own *will* and *pleasure* comes forth in such and such an *administration*, and goes out of *it*, and leaves it, and takes up *another*. And this is clear in all God's proceedings with the world, both in the *Jewish* Church and State; and *Christians* now. And Heb. 12. 26, 27. when God is gone out, and hath left such or such an *administration*, of what kind soever it is, be it *religious*, *moral*, or *civil;* such an *administration* is a *desolate house*, a *temple* whose *veil* is rent, a *sun* whose *light* is darkened; and to *worship* it then, is to *worship* an *Idol*, an *Image*, a *form*, without God, or any *manifestation* of God in it, save to *him*, who (as *Paul* saith) *knows an Idol to be* 1 Cor. 8. 4. *nothing.*

K 2

The *pure, spiritual, comprehensive* Christian, is one who grows up with God from *administration* to *administration*, and so walks with God in all his *removes* and *spiritual* increasings and *flowings;* and such are *weak* and in the *flesh* who tarry *behind*, worshipping that *form* or *administration* out of which God is departed.

Phil. 3. 14.
2 Cor. 3.
18.

A Postscript to Master Gataker, Author of a Book called Shadows without Substance, written against me.

SIR,

THE reasons why I did not answer you were these: I mean your last Book, called *Shadows without Substance, &c.*

I found that *Replies* and *Rejoinders* did exceedingly confound and perplex the *plainness* and *simplicity*, and *glory* of *Truth*, and had much of *self*, and *passion*, and *recrimination;* which I am confident the Lord will shew you in much of what you have written. For I am assured that God will reveal and convince you *powerfully* and *mightily* in many passages which *yourself* wrote, and not the *Spirit* of God. Lay your hand upon your heart, and consider sadly, if the *advantage* of the *times*, the *glory* of re*putation*, the *passion* of *man* in you, and the *multitude* of *years*, and *fame* of *learning* (not willing to be con*vinced* by *days* or *months*) did not write most of your last Book.

What you wrote in the *sincerity* of *Spirit*, and in that *measure* of *Truth* you received, I rejoice in; and what you wrote in the *artifice* of your *parts*, your *wit*, and your other *human advantages*, or devices of *flesh* and *blood*, whereby you laid on co*lours* to make your own *Arguments* fair and comely to a man judging no higher than *Reason*, or in your own *measure* of *Truth*, and whereby you laid on your *darker* and more *shadowish* stuff upon *me* your *adversary*, rendering me to the Reader, both in your *Title-page*, and throughout your *Book*, as one that denied the *Apostles'* Doctrine, and *Christ's*, because I denied your *conclusions* and *deductions* to be that very *Doctrine*, and the mind of those very *Scriptures* of Christ and the Apostles. This, I say, must pass under the *fiery trial*, and you must suffer *loss*, so as by *fire*.

Surely, to aeny what Master *Gataʀer*, or some *Synods* of *men* say, is not to deny what *Christ* and the *Apostles* say, unless the *Spirit* of God *reveal* in *them one* and the same *Truth*, and that they all speak by *one* and the *same Spirit*, in *one* and the *same language.*

Nor did I see that you in all your *Writings* had done anything against the *truth* declared by *me;* but had only defended *yourself*, and your own *measure* of *truth*, with re*jection* and *reproaches* of *mine;* and all this in the *form* only of *argumentation* and *confutation*, not in the *power:* so as I did *rest* without re*plying*, knowing that the *substance* of what *truth* I had *written* was as I had received then; and would *abide*, because he who is the *pattern* of all *truth*, Jesus Christ, *abides the same, yes-*

terday, and to-day, and for ever.
And for any *expressions* of mine, or
form of *words* which may make
truth appear to some not *one* and
the *same :* I only can as yet *speak*
truth in the *language* given me :
when I can speak more *tongues,*
or the *languages* of several *Chris-*
tians, of which the *gifts* of
tongues were a sign, then *I* and
you shall be better understood by
ourselves and *others.*

Sir, I have spoken one *particu-*
lar more *clearly,* which you and
some others spake on in my *Book.*
And thus I take my leave of *you,*
desiring to *love* any *appearance* of
God in you, and to forgive any *in-*
firmities in you, which are of *man ;*
as I desire *myself* to be *loved* or
forgiven of *others.*

And truly I do not *expound* that
of *contending earnestly for the*
Truth to be in *reproaches* and *pas-*
sions, in *Replies* and *Rejoinders,*
and many *Books ;* but in *Spirit,*
and *spiritual* affection, and pure
manifestation of the same *Truth.*

Sir, your Friend,

JOHN SALTMARSH.

A pretended Heresy.

In a
Book
called
*Hell
broke
loose.*

P. 84.

THAT which is *pretended*, or at least *believed* by some to be *Heresy* in my *Book of Grace,* is this; which I desire to explain more fully, that it may appear more clearly to be *Truth:*

That Christ hath believed perfectly, repented perfectly, mortified sin perfectly for us.

First. That Christ hath *done all* for us, is *truth:* he hath *fulfilled all righteousness,* both that righteousness which is of the *Law,* and that which is of the *Gospel,* in *graces, &c.* and upon this account *he is made unto us righteousness, &c.*

Secondly. *Faith, repentance, mortification,* were all in Christ *originally, primarily,* as in their *nature,* their *fountain,* their *root* or *seed;* and therefore he is said to give *repentance to Israel;* and he is *the author and finisher of our faith;* and it is called *the faith of the Son of God;* and *of his fulness have all we received, and grace for grace;* for every *grace in him,* a *grace in us.*

And to say *Christ* hath done all these for us, first in *himself*, and then in *us* through *himself*, I hope is such an *Heresy* as we all believe. It may be, my want of clearer explanation made it be taken for *Heresy;* which I hope will now be judged more candidly to be a *Truth.*

Nor can this (*That Christ hath all graces and perfection in himself*) prove that we stand in need of none in us, no *Faith* nor *Repentance* in us, nor *mortification of sin* in us, no more than *Paul's* Doctrine of *Grace* and *Faith*, and the *Christian* to be under *Grace*, destroy the *Law*, or make *void Faith*, or cause men to *sin that Grace may abound.*

I never yet denied the *Graces* and *Fruits* of the *Spirit* of God, which appear in *Faith*, *Repentance*, *new Obedience*, *Mortification of sin*, as may be seen in all *things* I have written. It may be I may speak *Truth* in such a *notion* or *conception*, or *measure* of *light* .as I have received it in, and not in *another's*. The *Christian*, as the *English* or French, can only speak in his *own Tongue* or *Lan-*

guage, till the *Lord be one, and his name one amongst us :* and in the mean time, let us judge *Heresy* by the *Truth* in *Scripture,* and in the *Spirit ;* not as it *seems* to us so, or appears so, perhaps not for want of *true light* in what is written but *more light* to what is already written, to make it more clearly appear *true light.*

To Master Knolls, the Author of a Book, called The shining of a flaming Fire, &c. written against me, as to the 'point of Baptism.

DEAR BROTHER,

I HAVE been long *silent,* not because what you wrote had prevailed in *me* to believe the Ordinance of *Baptism* by water, so practised, of that *necessity,* or of that *pure* and *Apostolic* practice in *these* times, since the *outward Court* given to the *Gentiles* hath been *trodden down,* and the *gifts* of *Spirit,* which was the *glory* and *life* of those *visible administrations* then, now taken away. But I was not very *hasty*, because I know it is not man that *teacheth Truth*, but God; *Ye shall be all taught of God.* There are *three* things I propound to *you*, with many *other*. John 6. 45.

1. That all that *baptize* now by the power of *teaching*, (*Go teach and baptize*) do *teach* in the same *gift* the *disciples* that *baptized* formerly did *teach;* that is, as the *oracles of God*, in the pure manifestation of the *Spirit* of God, else that Command, *Go teach and baptize*, belongs not to *disciples* o. less *pure*, less *certain*, and less *infallible teaching*, as all *disciples* now in *mystical Babylon;* or the *flesh*, are; but to disciples of the *first anointing*, or *first fruits* of the *Spirit*, such as the *Apostles* were, and such as *Philip* and *Ananias*, and the *brethren* with *Peter, &c.* Mat. 28.

2. That the *Baptism* of *water* is *Christ's Baptism*, or his *administration;* but it is *John's* and his *Ministery:* *I come baptizing with water; but he shall baptize you with the Holy Ghost:* And therefore *Christ* never gave it to his disciples in their first *Commission* to *preach* to the *Jews*, nor *bap-*

Mat. 10. *tized* he any *himself,* that can be
found; nor doth it appear that
this in *Matth.* 28, is meant of
baptizing by *water,* but by the
Spirit, or *baptism* of *gifts,* which
Christ baptized with in their *administration,* saying, *Lo, I am
with you,* or *in you, &c.*

3. That the *disciples* of *Christ
baptized* only by water, as in
John's Ministery, though into
Christ, as all *legal administrations* were, *viz.* to *Christ;* and
did it partly in honour to *John's*
Ministery, (for, *a greater prophet
than John hath not* risen) and to
the *believer's weakness;* as in that,
1 *Cor.* 1. *To the weak, I was weak: To
them under the Law, as under the
Law, &c.* yet, saith he, *I was not
sent to baptize:* It was no part of
his *Commission,* but of his *spiritual
liberty,* and to *edification* of the
weak : for he *circumcised.*

And there is another thing which
hath caused much mistake and *confidence* in this point of *Baptism* by
water, and that is, The not distin-
Rom. 6. guishing the *doctrine of Baptisms,*
Col. 2. but *interpreting* the *words* of *Baptism* used in the *Epistles,* which
appear to be words of *mystery,*

and spiritual *immersion*, as to the mysteries of God, and of being made by one *Spirit* one with *Christ*, one in his *death*, buried with him by *Baptism*, *&c.* to be of a mere *literal*, *elementary* significàtion, and to be meant of *water* only, and from this, *pressing* it as *necessary*, *&c.*

And further, there is no little mistake of that in the *Hebrews*, where the *doctrine of Baptisms* is reckoned amongst the *first principles* of the *doctrine* of Christ; whereas those *first principles* are reckoned in the *Hebrews*, not as if Heb. 6. all of them were things to be for ever the *principles* of every *Christian*, but of the *doctrine* of Christ in some of those things, as to that *age*; those things being first brought forth in that *ministration* of Christ' then: for if it were otherwise, and all they of *necessity* as the *first principles*, then where is the other *Baptism of gifts* there mentioned in the *Word?* For the Βαπτισ- word is *Baptisms*, not *Baptism*. μῶν διδα- And further, the Apostle rather Χῆς. calls *Christians* up *higher*, more into *Spirit:* Wherefore leaving, saith he, the *doctrine* of Christ,

Heb. 6. 1. *let us go on to perfection,* or *to*
that which is *perfect;* which is
Christ himself. As if he should
say, Let us be no more *weak Chris-*
tians, but such as seek *higher* and
more excellent things.

I refer you to the *Doctrine of*
Baptisms here in my *Book,* where
I have not *controversially* written,
but in *meekness,* and *plain dis-*
tinction of *things.*

Nor am I against Baptism by
water, if administered according
to the *measure of light* ye are under, and not in an *Apostolical ne-*
cessity and *pressure,* and as a *di-*
viding Ordinance to the *unity of*
the Spirit of God in *Christians.*

Dear Sir, I *love* and *tender*
those *true appearances* of God that
are in *you,* and rejoice with you
in beholding that *glory* by which
we are all *changed from glory to*
glory, &c. and am, your Friend and
Brother in the Lord,

JOHN SALTMARSH.

F I N I S.

J Whittingham 20 Tookes Court.

Printed by BoD™in Norderstedt, Germany

V.